I0143263

VISION
Accomplished
The Indigo Child Story

Elena Emma

Copyright © 2012 Elena Emma
All rights reserved.
ISBN-10: 0615752772
ISBN-13: 978-0615752778

To Mom & Dad
for creating me the way I am

To Max
for loving me as I am

To Alex Nester
for teaching me to embrace who I am

To Alec & Phil
for inspiring me to advance what I am

Contents

"When you don't fit into the world, create your own."

PROLOGUE

It was a gloomy November morning, around 10:30 am. The Starbucks was nearly empty, save for a few regulars, who had nothing else to do at this time of day but hit their favorite community coffee spot to catch up on reading, work, or gaming. Several baristas were flirting and telling each other half-true college success stories. In the corner of the store, at a small table tucked away under a tranquil coffee image, sat a couple in their late-20s-mid-30s. The man and the woman were arguing fairly loudly about something, but judging from their body language, they really loved each other. You know, the deep kind of love, the love that comes with years, tears shed, and smiles spent together, the love that has an aura of passion and connection far beyond the infatuation of jealousy and I-do-for-you-you-do-for-me nonsense. The couple was getting more and more intense in their exchange, when suddenly the man yelled at the woman, attracting attention of the nearby coffee drinkers. He then sank into his chair, and a tear rolled silently out of the corner of his eye. The woman didn't move. There was an abrupt, eternal silence between the two.

1

LOSING A DREAM

Hi. Her name is the Girl. She is a BooXkeeper. *BooXkeeper is the bookkeeper with passion and style.* BooXkeeper takes pride in the quality of work that she does, yet she uses her profession and earnings solely to lead a fulfilling, well-rounded life.

If you think that the Girl has always dreamt of being an accountant, juggling debits and credits day in and day out, you could not be further from the truth. Although many speculate that there are no accidents in life, only acts of fate, the Girl has ended up in the accounting field by the purest accident.

She has started her business degree at a community college. Ever since she was five, she imagined that she would have her own business, but that was the extent of her profound knowledge of what she wanted to do with her life when she grew up. As a child, she didn't know what field that business was supposed to be in. The Girl was planning to move out of her parents' house as soon as she turned 18 to regain some freedom, but by the time she turned 18, she felt crazily in love with a young man named Max, and decided that she wanted to move in with him. She felt unstoppable and delusional in her happiness, like all people in love, but to move in with the boyfriend, she needed money. There was no way in the world she was going to ask her parents for a financial support, so she needed a "real" job. At that time, HR Block was offering a 12 week tax preparer certification course, and she applied. Three months later, The Girl received the certificate, landed her first "real" job in a CPA office for a tax season, and moved out. For few years, she did tax preparation for the enrolled agent while working as a staff accountant in small to mid-size businesses, and finishing up college. She was good at whatever she touched whenever she really wanted it. As a result, the Girl got her first Controller title at the age of 20 and finished her Master's degree at the age of 21. At the same time, the enrolled agent that the Girl worked for throughout her school years invited her to come on as a junior partner, and offered to let the Girl buy out her tax practice, since the agent was planning to retire soon. The offer was more than appealing. It made perfect logical sense. It was a no brainer, right? Wrong. By the age of 21, with Masters in Accounting with Emphasis in Taxation, the Girl had enough experience in the field to know that accounting bored her to death. She wanted to explore, play, and get as far away from the accounting field as she could. Indeed, she hated the accounting she knew. Can you blame the Girl for her desire to have fun at such a young age? So she declined the offer to buy out the practice, and took a detour in her professional life.

Fast forward five years and several business endeavors: the Girl got married (to the same boyfriend she moved in with when she turned 18), and after the birth of their second child she opened up an event planning/design company. *This was her vision*. The emotional fulfillment was there, the people factor, the creativity, the growth, the interest, the spark, and the passion. It was almost perfect... except for the money. She had neither the money from the business activities to sustain the business and take a regular salary nor the money to invest in the development of the business. Besides, the family resources was slowly drifting away. First, the unemployment was gone, then all savings disappeared, followed by the 401k. Max started panicking. His service business was only two years old and wasn't bringing in enough profit to support the whole family. His prior financial background and Bachelor Degree were obsolete and wouldn't get him a decent full-time job. So he was forced to face two completely unacceptable, yet unavoidable facts: on one hand, he promised his wife that she could work on developing her dream event planning business while he, as a provider and protector of the family, offered financial support; on the other hand, there was not enough money to feed the family. Ironically, the Girl was the only one who could get a full-time job, because of her Masters in Accounting and her hands-on experience in the field.

On that gloomy November morning in Starbucks, Max and the Girl were arguing about the lack of money, bills, and other unpleasant matters that took their toll by stealing the energy from an otherwise great relationship. This wasn't the first discussion on the subject, but this time Max had just come from the bank, where he exchanged their final saving deposit for a cashier's check to pay the rent. There were no more savings left: that was the end. The argument went back and forth for over an hour as the Girl refused to believe there were no more funds available. Helplessly, she went over the same scenarios seeking a possible solution. As time passed, the conversation heated up, and suddenly, out of desperation, her husband yelled at the top of his lungs.

"What do you suggest, Girl? I don't know what to do. We need at least $10,000 per month to cover our expenses between kids, schools, after-school activities, household, insurance, food, and rent. I can't get a job because I've got no credentials. *You can get a job, but you choose not to!*" And the tears started rolling from his eyes.

No doubt, it's always an uneasy sight to see someone you love cry. It's even more difficult when it's a strong man that you absolutely and unconditionally adore. The Girl sat down, and remained glued to her chair for an hour. Then she got up to go home, but stayed in the car in the driveway for a long period, sobbing, unable to go on with what seemed to be manageable just few hours ago. These are the moments that, as people say, either make you or break you, yet when they come, it feels like the whole world stops spinning. These moments feel like a little death.

When the Girl saw Max crying, her heart started bleeding. She quickly realized that no dream in the world (event planning felt like a dream at that moment) was worth her husband's tears. She also knew that at this point only she could save their family. About four months ago, she came across a book by Jeannette Walls called *The Glass Castle*. One of the characters in the book, Jeanette's mother Rose Walls, was a true artist. She enjoyed the process of creation for the sake of creation and completely despised all the rules. She would frequently withdraw into her own world where she could play with art, however, she left her children unattended and starved, pushing them to figure out for themselves how to make money and where to get food and clothing. While the mom was addicted to adventure, art, and excitement, the kids were growing up completely abandoned and unhappy. The Girl saw a lot of herself in the character of Rose, as we often do when we transpose ourselves into the world of the book, and at that point she promised herself that she would never be "Rose" to her children. Apparently, now was the time to prove it, and she wasn't going to fail that test as her life depended on it.

The only option the Girl had to resolve the situation was to give up her dream, get a full-time job in the accounting field she hated, and sacrifice everything she had ever desired for the sake of the family. *But how do you give up a dream without breaking some part within yourself?* All of this was so against her core, that she became instantaneously depressed. She had not only lost her vision, but she also lacked a suitable resume or legit skills to work full-time. *This was her reality.*

When someone tells you that the best person who can give you advice is yourself, don't believe that person. He has never been in the situation of a complete disaster when you are entirely alone, at the bottom, completely lost in the translation of your own destiny, in a mental coma, and *any sound piece of information that would kick you out of the zombie state one way or another is sincerely appreciated. That sound piece of information is called advice.* And you should be forever grateful if you have a person in your life who *can* give you advice, because you never know when you may need it.

The Girl was lucky. She had just the right person to turn to. Alex was her long time friend and mentor in his late thirties. He was a completely unconventional and unpredictable man, with a post-Soviet background, who was also one of the most influential contemporary personal and business consultants in the country. As any gifted man, Alex had a combination of what society would describe as superb and horrific character traits, but to the Girl, he had two main advantages. First, he was extremely knowledgeable on a million of different subjects, and could carry on deep philosophical discussions with logical proofs and creative, simple examples for hours and hours, bringing the learning experience to a completely new level of comprehension. Second, Alex also was the only person in the world that could objectively explain the Girl to herself in a plain language with down-to-earth detailed analysis and absence of judgment. The latter skill was the one that she could use the most right now.

"Alex, Max wants me to go get an accounting job," the Girl cried hysterically as soon as he picked up the phone. She knew that she didn't have to explain herself, or say hello for that matter. With Alex she shared an unspoken and immediate understanding. It was easy to be herself. In fact, he was one of a handful of people with whom she could turn off any internal filters.

"Why now?" Alex sounded calm and collected.

After all, he did personal crisis management for a living, at which he was freakishly and originally amazing. The man had a style of his own.

"No money. We ran out of money… is this how my dream ends? Is that my fucking "happy" ending?"

"Come tomorrow, we'll talk."

"Why tomorrow?" She asked, stunned. She thought she was on the verge losing her mind and she needed help yesterday, not tomorrow.

"Because when you are weeping, I am talking to your tears. I prefer to have a conversation with you. Tomorrow you will be yourself again, and the talk will be a lot more productive."

***

Twenty eight hours later, the Girl was sitting in the backyard of the small duplex where Alex lived with his girlfriend, warming up by the fire pit and drinking green tea. She wasn't crying anymore. She was numb inside, just a shade of her normal self.

"But I hate routine accounting. I was running away from it for so long. How do I go back now to something that I despise so much?"

"When you know your strengths and weaknesses, and you stay true to yourself, you can go into any field. Learn yourself: what can you and can't you do? How do you do it? Why do you do it? How long does it take you? What drives you? What's your attention span? Be honest, because the more you know about yourself, the easier it will be to package all that information in a simple but significant life formula and then apply it to whatever you do. In this particular case, you will just apply it to the field of accounting."

"Why accounting?"

"Because you need the most efficient and the fastest solution to resolve your monetary problems. Going back to the accounting field is that solution. You have the degree, the experience; therefore, the barriers to entry for you are minimal. It's logical to choose the highway to jumpstart this particular journey, instead of searching for village roads, as picturesque as they may appear."

"But accounting is boring. I will go crazy, and it will eventually break me."

"Remember: *Something can only break you if you allow it to break you.* Don't allow that to happen. Instead, any time you feel out of sorts, remember to stay true to yourself."

"True to what self? To the girl who can't concentrate on one task for more than 2 to 5 hours at a time and then she needs to switch her focus entirely? To the girl who has a hard time following any rules or procedures, has a potential case of Attention Deficit Disorder, and zero desire to participate in office politics? The girl, who somehow never fits in the societal margins, because she asks "why" and questions the authority that was given, but not earned? Are you kidding me? With a bouquet like this, I won't last a day in any office, despite of how fast I learn and pick up on the fly. I am setting myself up for a failure from the start."

"I think you are exaggerating," Alex put more logs in the fire pit. "Because you refuse, at the moment, to look at yourself positively. All I am saying is that when things get tough, keep in mind to *stay true to yourself.* Only then you won't break."

"Staying true to myself. Easier said than done. If I were completely true to myself, I would say: Screw the job. I don't want to work for anybody, and even less so I want to be an accountant again." The Girl was rambling in her thoughts later that night on her way home, looking through the drops of water on her windshield, knowing in her gut that she didn't have the luxury to make this bold statement out loud, because at this point, she didn't have a choice. She could neither bear the thought of Max being as upset as he was the day before, nor to be in peace with the fact that her kids might not be able to have a good dinner or participate in fun activities. When she was getting her Masters, she would always half-jokingly say that she was getting it for a rainy day, and she would only use it if she had a hard time finding other resources to feed her kids. That rainy day had come (literally).

Alex was right, accounting was the fastest and the most efficient solution to the current problem, and this time she needed to opt out for the obvious resolution. Although, she didn't know where to start, she had no time to sit around and wait. It was time to whip up that old resume, bite her tongue, hope for a miracle, and start looking for a job.

2

BOOT CAMP

Everywhere the Girl turned she hit a wall. Her resume was good, but not strong enough for the corporate world. Her corporate friends couldn't help her with a job because she hadn't had enough corporate experience. Besides, let's face it: she wasn't the "corporate type." Same friends told her she was too air-headed and incapable of sustaining stable, long-term commitments, and therefore they couldn't refer her. In their worlds their reasoning made complete sense: she was rebellious and unreliable; switching jobs every 1.5-2 year to look for new opportunities. How could they associate their name with this referral, when it could potentially jeopardize their careers? Why should they take this unnecessary risk?

She turned to job hunters, but their answer wasn't any different.

"I've been in the industry for over 15 years, and I can tell you with certainty that your resume is not sellable," one job hunter said at the interview, shaking her head. "You have way too much small business experience, not enough longevity on every job, and the experience you've obtained from these positions is completely irrelevant for task-oriented corporate departments. It will be very complicated to explain why all of sudden you are looking to make a switch into a big company, and how they can trust that you will stay there for good. It's too much work for the recruiter to push your resume."

"But if my resume was a clear cut case and the process of finding the job was straightforward, I would do it myself without engaging your services. Isn't that why other people come to the job-hunters? Because they have a convoluted situation and they can't do it themselves?" the Girl asked with annoyance. She realized that these questions were not exactly "appropriate" for the interview, however this was the 5th interview in the last week with no result, and she was growing tired of the same answers.

"The other people come to the job-hunters because they need a job," the recruiter smiled at her.

"But I *need* a job, I am willing to start right away, part-time, full-time, or temporary. I work fast and diligently, I will be one of the best hires that your clients may have ever had."

"Other people have strong resumes, so it's easy to match them with the hiring companies. *You don't match.*" The recruiter looked at her watch, signaling the conversation was over. "In any case, go through the standardized series of tests on software expertise and theoretical accounting comprehension, and we'll see what we can find for you in the future. End of November is not a good time for changing jobs, because everyone is tied up with budgets and getting ready to close out the year. But I am sure suitable openings may show up in end of January or February. I will see that the front desk schedules your professional testing in the next few days."

The Girl left the recruiter's office, passed by the front desk, and went straight to the elevator. There was no point in scheduling anything further. She had already taken a few of these tests within the last week, and learned quickly that they were completely outdated and immaterial to today's business world. Seriously, who cared about QuickBooks 2000, basic Excel 2003, manual journal posting, and the elementary definition of wages? How come, with all this new technology and innovation, there were no questions on any add-on applications that integrate with QuickBooks products or alternative cloud solutions? Wasn't that more pertinent? Spending two hours on these tests was an absolute waste of time. Besides, the recruiters couldn't offer her a reasonable salary. What they considered reasonable for the skill set she possessed was not going to cover her minimum expenditures—not even close. Nor did she have a few months to wait until jobs became available at the end of January or February, because no one was *statistically* hiring during November or December. And truthfully, even if she magically landed an interview with a large corporation, she would completely fail the prearranged process of multi-layer interviews, pages-long applications, and personality/skill testing as a result of her lack of experience, bluntness, and lack of proper corporate interviewing skills. She knew she needed to find an alternative solution.

The Girl turned to professional job hunting websites. All major sites like monster.com, jobhunter.com, hotjobs.com, and a dozen others proved to be the extension of the recruiter hiring process with the same job lists. But then: there was Craigslist. Craigslist was (and still is) the only job-hunting (or in fact, everything-hunting) website that seemed like a live wire which connected the business and personal world with the reality, efficiency and the speed of the XXI century. This site was as present-day as it got. And though the spread of jobs, compensation and hiring companies' offers were often so wide that applying for a position seemed like playing Russian roulette, at least there was variety, hope, and fast response time. For the next two weeks the Girl dwelled in the magic kingdom of Craigslist. Every morning she would send 50 resumes or more, and every 15 minutes she would check her e-mail for updates. She was applying for any position available that involved accounting, and as a result, she finally started getting real calls from real companies, for interviews for real jobs. Wheels started to turn.

The interviews are always a personality fit test: you are being tested whether you will mentally, physically, and professionally fit the interviewer and his personal objectives for the position you are being hired for. Some of the Girl's interviews were short, sweet and productive; others were long, boring, and occasionally completely out of whack.

Once she was invited to interview with a health product company. The controller was sizing her up and down, drilling her on the technical knowledge of the subject, the diversity of her experiences, etc. After an hour of intense conversation, everything seemed to be going well. The Girl felt like she was acing all the questions, until all of sudden the controller popped one more question.

"Girl, your resume and your skill set seem to be perfect for this job. What is wrong with you?"

"What do you mean?" She asked politely hopeful that she had misunderstood the question.

"I mean, you are an amazing candidate. Something has to be wrong with you. What is it?"

The Girl was perplexed and pissed. "Why does this man think that if I am great at what I do, something has to be wrong with me? *Why do all these people think that something is wrong with me?*" She took a long moment to catch her breath and pretend that she was looking for a sophisticated answer.

"I am crazy," she replied slowly. "That's what's wrong with me."

"And how do you deal with stress?"

"I get behind the wheel of my convertible and drive at 100 mph until I feel refreshed."

Obviously, she didn't get this job. But honestly, nothing had felt as invigorating to her in the last few weeks as the instant when she slowly walked out of the controller's office, taking her sweet time to recline the roof of her Volvo C70 right in front of his window, turning on loud, liberating music, and rolling lazily out of the parking lot, enjoying perfect, sunny, 70-degree California weather in the middle of Wednesday. It was a silent revolt: the subconscious denial to agree with the common belief that something had to be wrong with her in order to be accepted anywhere, including this company.

***

The one who searches with the determination of a lion shall always find.

One evening around 8 pm, the Girl got an unexpected phone call from a CPA who was looking for a temporary tax season employee. They talked briefly, and he invited her for an interview the next day.

Walter Diggins CPA firm was located in the heart of an older busy business area. The office occupied multiple rooms in a building built in the late 1980's, and everything inside and outside looked, felt, and smelled twenty years old. The office consisted of four offices for managers, a large open space for the rest of the staff, and a storage room.

"This place needs a major face lift," the Girl noted to herself in the waiting room, while a charming dark-haired woman in her late fifties left the desk to inform the partner of her arrival.

Walter Diggins was a tall, slender, grey-haired man in his late sixties, who had the solid fat stamp of accomplishment and significance on his face. He sat the Girl down on a worn leather black sofa, barely glanced over her resume, and started talking. He went on for 40 minutes about how her only real advantage was her Masters degree in Taxation, how green she was, how little hands-on experience she might have since she was so young, how she could become a perfect auditor in five to seven years if she committed herself to doing the same tasks over and over until complete perfection, and how he was ready to save her from the mistakes she was about to make and to help her build herself up as a solid CPA as the time passed. The Girl kept quiet the whole time. She didn't have the strength to argue that before Walter could judge her expertise on any subject, he should have at least asked some applicable questions. She didn't tell him that she could potentially bring more relevant knowledge to his construction clients, who were his specialty, than some of his staff, because she actually ran a construction company with fifty to ninety employees with her husband for three years. And she didn't point out that she had no interest in doing audit work because it was dreadfully tedious. It didn't matter anymore. Her energy and her confidence were running thin. None of her past achievements mattered here; neither did her personality. She was drained and in desperate need of a miracle. The fact that she didn't have to converse, as long as she nodded every few minutes, allowed her to distance herself and withdraw mentally from the conversation, thus staying neutral and letting the other party believe whatever he wanted to believe. After the monologue was over, Walter asked her when she was ready to start and said that she was hired. Four weeks into the job search, the Girl had a temporary, seasonal, full-time, decently-paying accounting job. Woohoo.

***

The Walter Diggins office was a perfect place to learn: ultra-conservative, structured with a three-layered review process for any document before it made it out the door. The Girl wasn't allowed to have any flexibility or do any mind-engaging work. As a newbie in the company, despite of her skills and knowledge, she had to start with basics and stick with basics for the longest time until she was allowed to do something vaguely more involved. There were procedures for everything: how to open the file, how to close the file, how to operate the file, how to analyze the file, how to look at the file, and even how to think about the file; how to talk to the client when he came to the office for his tax appointment, how to act when he stopped by to pick up the reports, how to call a client for any additional information. Procedures were everywhere, any step taken within the company had to be documented and put in a form of procedure to be later distributed among fellow employees. Everybody had to follow the procedures, even if they decreased efficiency. The hours and responsibilities were strictly set with reporting controls, which were described in additional procedures. Sometimes, the Girl seriously wondered whether there was a procedure on how to eat lunch and use the bathroom as well, and she just mysteriously missed it.

Walter turned out to be somewhat chauvinistic and ego-centric, but very dedicated, diligent and knowledgeable in an old-school way. He was very full of himself, teaching the employees to practice "mental jiu-jitsu" with the clients, like he did. Every time he made his weekly rounds, Walter would walk around the office and call the staff "the troopers", possibly imagining he was a military general who led his troops into the short and bloody January-through-April war with uncompleted tax returns and deadlines. The latest hire was doing the least interesting work, like the filing, the document paper trail, the checklists, the follow ups on the checklists, etc. Credentials didn't matter; neither did effectiveness. To the Girl, this whole setup felt like she had entered boot camp. She needed to do her initiation term to gain respect from those of higher rank, because in this world, the world of Walter Diggings, everything had to be earned from the bottom up. Opting for a shortcut would be considered a disgrace.

The people in the office were nice but also extremely conservative. *In the small business arena, the staff personalities, beliefs, and energy levels often reflect those of the owner.* The office staff consisted of several mothers, whose husbands worked in large corporations and were hooked for life with benefit packages and endless vacations. Their wives took this job for seasonal income while their kids went to school. Other staff members included a few young guys, who worked full-time throughout the year, but had barely any life interests outside of the office. No one was passionate about what they did, but they did it anyway.

The Girl quickly realized it would be awfully hard to survive in this environment, because it was the exact opposite of everything she appreciated in the world of business, professionalism, and people. Besides, in reality, there would be no exciting project in the near future. She was not detail oriented, and therefore was incapable of memorizing all the tables, dates, numbers, legislations, and tax rates, which meant that she would never become a good CPA or auditor. Moreover, she was physically only productive and effective for 2 to 5 hours a day, so she worked extremely fast to finish everything during this timeframe. However, she had to stay in the office from 9 am until 5 pm, just like everybody else, and was bound to wasting a lot of precious time she would rather spend with her boys. There was really nothing to look forward to in this office, nothing to stimulate her mind to its fullest capacity. In order to get up every morning and go to work, she had to learn to love what she was doing: the mundane, repetitive tasks that were somewhat interesting first time around due to their novelty, yet completely boring after that.

When things get tough, stay true to yourself.

The Yoga Sutras of Patanjali, Hindu scripture and the foundational text of Yoga, teaches the practice of surrender to the Higher Source (Ishvara Pranidhana). Ishvara Pranidhana is a "big picture" yoga practice: It initiates a sacred shift of perspective that helps human beings to remember, align with, and receive the grace of being alive. Many modern Westerners have only experienced surrendering to a higher source as a last resort, when they have confronted seemingly insurmountable problems. But in the Yoga Sutra, Patanjali transforms "surrender" from this emergency response into an essential ongoing practice.

For the Girl, in order to survive this period of her life, she needed to surrender to a deep and profound understanding that while she was building her own life, controlling it and taking full responsibility for the outcome, everything on a bigger scale had been preset by the Universe (or God, depending on religious preferences). Every step, occurrence, challenge, or person that she met on this journey was part of a pre-existing, strategic plan for something much bigger than she could ever imagine. That understanding, the blind conviction that everything always happened for a reason, would be the only source of energy that would help her stay true to herself.

In her memory, the Girl returned to her college years, and tried to remember why she liked accounting in the first place. There had to be a spark somewhere in the beginning that kept her going for quite a few years during and after school. She remembered that she was always fond of analyzing tax returns. Tax preparation was about people: what they did and what lifestyle they lead within a certain tax bracket. So she started with that. She discovered that entrepreneurship was a virus, a non-curable disease, and once a person opened more than one business venture, he was sick with this disease for life. She was also mesmerized by the social statistic that the majority of business owners in their mid 40s or early 50s were buying Porsches as soon as they could afford them. Was that the status call of that generation?

Some of the Girl's discoveries were down-to-earth and business-oriented. For example, in order to entertain herself, she started looking for niches within the office, analyzing the gaps and the possibilities of what was done, how it was done, at what capacity, and with what results. Here she found a tendency of business owners to pay more money for CPA services when they didn't have good bookkeepers. Yet, bookkeeping required no responsibilities other than basic accounting and business knowledge.

Bookkeeping could be outsourced and reviewed at a reasonable rate. Different industries had different specifications, which added to the variety of the bookkeeping process. And the variety added longevity to a mind frame like the Girl's. This is how the first seed was planted in what would later grow into BooXkeeping, a cutting edge bookkeeping company.

Other discoveries were allegoric. One of the most unusual ones that the Girl stumbled upon during her regular mind escapes was the fact that the account reconciliation process greatly resembled the sexual act. Here is this accountant, who tries to fit debits and credits together to get to a common plausible resolution. First, she goes gently over every little detail on the debit side, massaging and reviewing each transaction. Then, she does the same on the credit side. As the transactions check off, she is getting closer and closer to tying them to the correct balance. The further she falls into this playful process, the more she finds out about every transaction, and the closer she gets to the climax of this reconciliation. But as soon as all items are checked off based on the list, she discovers that, despite the rules and checklists, the difference between both sides still does not equal to zero. Now she needs to use an alternative approach to finish the reconciliation. How different is this from sexual foreplay? You wine, dine, undress, caress, hit all erogenous spots that are described in every angle in all popular magazines, and it seems that you are doing everything right, yet in the moment of expectation, when you think you are about to hit a volcano, you get the least expected result and the climax is not there. Something is just... missing. So this aroused/annoyed accountant starts to look for a strategy, for a trend. At this point she still thinks logically about the whole process, she is still optimistic and is simply looking for a mistake in the algorithm. As the time goes by to no effect, the accountant, who is now heavily sweating, gives up on the logic and starts to fantasize and to play with numbers. She is adding and subtracting them in a frenzy, looking for a signal, a hint, a sign. And then, when she is drained and practically hopeless, there is this sudden message on the screen "Congratulations, your reconciliation difference is zero. Proceed to printing the reconciliation reports?" BOOM! The accountant loses control, screams at the top of her lungs, throws her arms into the air, and performs a wild victory dance that resembles the orgasm convulsions. There it is, the climax of the reconciliation process, a short and bright feeling of being unstoppable and on the top of the world!

Now, does every accountant get to this point? No. *Just like in sex, the true force behind the passion which leads to a cosmic experience is the integrity of the process.* Many accountants get tired and give up too early, writing off small or significant differences between both sides of the account, thus reconciling, but cheating themselves out of the beautiful sentiment of the honest conquest. Of course, no accountant will ever admit to faking it. Neither do millions of people during their sexual encounters.

***

The Girl didn't make friends in the office. Neither did she make enemies. The moms would come in the morning and be gone by 2 pm. At 2 pm, the Girl's mind would shut off and go into airplane auto-pilot mode. The only people left in the room were two guys who worked full-time. One of them was the Girl's *open wall cubicle* neighbor (what else can you politely call two desks crammed together, where employees face each other the entire day, without mention of personal space?).

Chan was a single Korean man in his early thirties with an extreme negative energy. He was a perfectionist who sliced his peanut butter sandwich in 10 perfect cubes, boxed them up in two separate containers and ate them at his table for breakfast and lunch. He would start his day with the phrase "Is it time to go home yet?" and he would religiously repeat it at least 15 times a day. He had been with the Walter Diggins CPA for over four years, and while he knew quite a lot and was very helpful at times, he would complain and nag about every little thing.

"Get ready," he warned the Girl in her first week. "In about a month you will not have time to breath, let alone have a life."

The Girl wasn't planning to give up on her life or stop breathing while performing the noble deed of accounting, so sitting next to Chan for eight hours a day every day was... well, a torture.

One day in the early February, the Girl came to work dead-tired and slightly agitated. She didn't have the strength to give up her event planning business since it was the only source of non-family related pleasure that she had, and so she continued to work weddings and birthdays on the weekends, while working full-time for Walter Diggins. This Monday marked her sixth week without a single day off, and the load had started to take its toll on her emotional well-being. Chan was especially "charming" that day. His grandma was in the hospital, and while his mind was probably with her, he whined and complained about the littlest inconveniences: the coffee was cold, the pencil was not sharpened, the computer worked slowly, the printer was cluttered, the office smelled of Indian food, the receptionist was picky, and so on. By the mid-day, the Girl was ready to strangle him.

"Chan," she made every effort to stay calm. "What makes you happy?"

"What do you mean?" He looked at her like she was a lunatic. "Nothing makes me happy."

"I see that clearly," she said with a sigh. "But if there was one thing that would make you happy, what would it be? What do you love, Chan?"

"I... I... I love... cakes. There you go. Cakes make me happy."

"Perfect, what is your favorite cake?"

"Why?" He was still looking at her like she needed psychiatric help. "Are you going to buy me a cake?" He was trying to be funny, but didn't know how to do it right.

"Yes, Chan, I will buy you a cake. In fact, I will be buying you a cake every Friday hoping that it will lighten you up. What is your favorite cake?"

"Red velvet," Chan replied, battling a feeling that this was surreal; that he was being set up.

Three days later, on Friday, the Girl walked into the office with a grocery bag and placed it on Chan's table.

"Here is your Red Velvet Cake. Bon Appétit!" She smiled at him.

"You *actually bought me* a cake?" He still couldn't believe his eyes.

"Yes, Chan. I promised you a cake, and I keep my promises. You can even eat it," she smirked at him. "But on one condition."

"I knew it! What do you want?"

"Every time you get yourself a piece of this cake, you have to say what *you are happy about today*. That's it. Quite simple, I think. You do that, and I will keep supplying the cakes for you to maintain your happiness. Do we have a deal?" She extended her right hand, waiting for a confirmatory shake.

"Yes, we have a deal." Chan shook her hand, still looking at her like he couldn't decide whether she was a dangerous hybrid between a psycho and a clown, or just plain stupid.

A few hours later, Chan circled around with the cake in his hand.

"Oh, I see you're craving some sweets. How cool! So what are you happy about today, Chan?" She looked at him with the innocent, curious expression of a five-year old.

"Nothing," he replied.

"I'm sorry," she was trying to stay neutral. "But I'm afraid you can't have this cake then. You agreed to the rules, and shook on it. Aren't you a man of your word? Please put the plate down, until you're ready to share what you're happy about. And remember,

I'm not looking for grand details of your private life. Anything goes."

Chan put the cake slice back into the fridge and didn't touch it for three days. Finally, three days later, after lunch, he came back from the kitchen with another slice of cake in his hand.

"Oh, I see you decided to give it another try. What are you happy about today?" She didn't move, but pierced him with her eyes.

"Gee, I thought you would forget about it by now." He looked nervously around his desk. "I am happy... I am happy...," suddenly his eyes stopped on an adding machine. "I am happy that this adding machine is working fine because the one before it was chewing the paper."

"Awesome! This is a great start! Enjoy your cake!" With these words, she gave him a hug and turned away.

Next Friday the Girl placed another cake on Chan's table. This time it was a three-layer chocolate mousse cake from the French bakery.

"Thought you would like to expand your dessert pallet," she said jokingly.

"What is that?" A colleague asked, passing by their desks.

"Oh, it's Chan's cake." The Girl was quick to answer.

"It's a cake for everybody." He added with frustration.

"Girl, did you bring it?" The colleague continued. "Don't you know that you've just violated Item # 3 from our new office procedures, that were presented by Walter at yesterday's meeting?"

"No, I didn't know. What's item # 3?" The Girl was out the day before because she needed to take her son to the doctor, so she missed the meeting.

"Here it is." Chan happened to have the document right on top of his client's file. "Item # 3: Eat healthy and responsibly. Avoid junk and comfort food, sweets, caffeine, and other types of snacks that may be harmful to your immediate well-being."

"Well, I'll pretend I haven't seen this." The Girl winked at the colleague mischievously. "After all, it's been statistically proven that *chocolate makes people happy.*" She smiled at Chan and proceeded to the kitchen to get freshly brewed coffee.

As every secret in any small office, the story about Chan's cake soon became widely known to everybody. What started off as a prank between the Girl and Chan had soon evolved into an office-wide game. Everyone wanted to participate in the "happy cake experience," so every time they sliced a piece of cake they would share what they were happy about on that day. The Girl just kept supplying the cakes. Did it shift the conformist mentality in the office into an everlasting utopia of happiness? Absolutely not. But at least this weekly game temporarily elevated the mood in the office.

One night after the dinner, the Girl shared this story with Max. She was washing the dishes and having a casual conversation with him about nothing and everything at the same time. She found this whole "happy cake" thing awfully cute, so she was excited to tell him all about it.

"The Girl, you are like a Village Idiot to them!" Max said lovingly, finishing his glass of wine.

"You know what?" The Girl put a plate back into the sink, turned off the water, and looked at him, her eyes very serious and sad. *"I'd much rather be a Village Idiot than a faceless dull accountant who doesn't have time to breath."*

***

The days in the office crawled by at a snail's pace. When someone tells you that the time goes by faster with age, don't believe them. It really depends on what you do with this time. Time, like anything else, is a matter of perception and changes depending on how you spend it and with what outcome.

Everything in the Girl's life was as airy and thick as London fog. It was the middle of March; the contract would soon be over, and she needed to figure out what to do with her professional life. She had a conversation with Walter about her future in the office. Walter confirmed in his lecture-like manner that he didn't have a full-time opportunity for her at the moment, but he could provide her with occasional contract work as a junior auditor for several weeks within the next nine months. He also mentioned matter-of-factly that if she were to stay with him for the next three to five years on a seasonal basis, she could count on a solid 10-15% salary increase by the end of this period, though that would depend on annual reviews. Until then, she was bound to make no more than $70,000 annually, no matter what she might imagine. Of course, if she got a CPA license, more experience in the field, and sufficient audit hours, the financial situation might change a little, just like it did for everyone before her and would for everyone after her. In other words, she had a preset ceiling limiting her professional and financial potential.

When she walked out of Walter's office, the Girl realized that although she was extremely grateful to Walter that she had a job at all, it was time to move on. A part of her was tired and anxious because for a short period of time, she finally had some stability in her life. Unfortunately, she hated every second of that stability as it was sucking the energy out of her with routine tasks, stipulated eight-hour days, exhausting procedures, ineffective meetings, and many other typical attributes of corporate work. On the other hand, she had no idea where to go from here, what position to apply for, what direction to choose. *She felt blindfolded, but at least her hands weren't tied.* Her emotions reminded her of dining in the dark on Valentine's Day (the Girl came upon the idea conducting research for one of her event-planning clients, and finally had the opportunity to go out and try it with Max).

If you have never dined in the dark, you have missed a mind-altering and the life-changing experience. You are invited to a pitch-black dining room for a pre-made dinner. You are served by a highly-trained blind or visually impaired staff who guide you along the way. You don't see a thing. Nothing! The dining in the dark experience is a great trust and acceptance exercise. You can't find your way to your table or to the restroom without the support of a guide, but your consciousness is battling the fact that not only you can't see a thing but neither can your guides. In order to move forward and relax, you just have to let go of the fear of lack of control, and completely unconditionally trust people you don't know — ultimately trusting the world around you. You also need to learn to accept the fact that although these people may be limited in certain skills, like vision, they are otherwise *masters of their realm*. Many people are bothered by the fact that they are served by disabled individuals, because it makes them uncomfortable and self-conscious, instead of being appreciative that they are invited into somebody else's world where they can humbly see what the other people see (which is, in this case, complete darkness), but most importantly they can feel what those people feel. The way you react to this experience is completely personal. However, once you give in to the inevitability of the present and let yourself unwind, the magic happens: whereas your vision is completely blocked and shut off, all your other senses take over: auditory and sensory controls kick in. You tap into a bottomless diversity of smells, sounds, voices, tastes, and textures! The imagination takes off on an untamed ride, making this dinner an unforgettable experience.

For the Girl, her life resembled complete darkness at the moment. Yet she knew deep in her gut that she strangely felt more at home in this blackness and chaos, trusting that everything would work itself out in due time, than she did in the prearranged comfort of a highly structured office. She did know for sure that she didn't like it when someone imposed a ceiling on her capabilities, which meant only one thing: she needed to start interviewing again.

3

MEN & NUMBERS

So the Girl have updated her resume with her current job experience, and started to look for a part or full-time contract. She still worked full-time at Walter Diggins office, and Max, who felt responsible and a little guilty for the whole process, offered to act as her job hunter. They were a team again. He took her resume, and just like she did back in November, help her apply daily to as many accounting jobs as there were available on Craigslist. The Girl was now open to the possibility of getting a few simultaneous part-time contracts. She believed this option could add a variety to her life, and thus she might finally learn to be at peace with accounting. After numerous interviews and phone calls, two part-time contracts came along. One of them would later evolve into the first BooXkeeping client, while the other one would turn into the cornerstone of the Girl's professional maturity.

The first contract rolled around in the end of March. A high-end real estate agent was looking for a bookkeeper who was able to go back into an unfinished set of books, close out the prior year, and move forward with weekly bookkeeping tasks. Faroukh Gazeri, who called himself Freddie, had gone through five bookkeepers in the course of six months. He had no idea where the paperwork was, and how it was supposed to be filed. He scheduled two interviews back to back with the Girl and her counterpart, but the candidate who Freddie was originally inclined to hire never made it to the interview. Instead, the Girl showed up. So she got the job, due to the time crunch of finishing the accounting tasks before the end of tax season. Or due to the destiny.

The other contract was for a part-time controller in a start-up product distribution company. One March evening, Max was sending the Girl's resume as usual when he found this particular ad, so he sent the resume there as well without a second thought. Around 8pm the Girl's cell phone rang. Generally, Max has never picked up her phone because he knew how adamant she was about her privacy. But this time the Girl was upstairs with the kids, and due to some unexplainable inclination he answered it.

"Good evening, may I speak with Girl?" There was a male voice on the other side.

"Yes, hold on one second, please," Max answered. He put the cell phone on mute and went upstairs. The Girl had fallen asleep on their son's bed while listening to his reading. Between the office and the events, she was working non-stop, and was very tired.

"Girl, it's for you. I think it's about work." He woke her up.

"Go away," she mumbled in a sleep. "What work at 8pm? Are you drunk? I'm not going to talk to anybody. I'm exhausted."

But Max didn't listen to her, he pressed mute again on the cell and shoved the phone to her.

"This is Girl," she answered trying her best to wake

up.

"Hi, Girl. My name is Jake Hutchinson, you have just sent me your resume about an hour ago."

"I sent you my resume about an hour ago?" She didn't touch the computer since she came home from work, so she looked at Max with a question. Max shrugged. " Oh yeah, I have sent so many resumes out in the last few hours. I apologize, but would you please remind me the name of your company?"

"It's Universal Distributions LLC. I am looking for a part-time controller. Would you be available for an interview tomorrow? My partner and I are leaving in the evening and we would like to meet with you before that."

"I am available at 8am, if that suits you," she answered.

"Perfect." They agreed to meet in the Starbucks closest to both parties.

The next morning, the interview went well. Jake was actually interested in her prior controller and self-employment experience more than her degree. The company was two years old and profitable. He needed someone to take over day-to-day accounting on a part-time basis, but also to build some kind of inventory system, develop business procedures, and to stay with the company while it was growing .The part-time job meant flexibility. The inventory system integration meant temporary full-time, mentally engaging work. Besides, for the first time in a very long while the Girl had a feeling she was talking to a sensible person who *understood* what modern business was all about. Except for the wicked fact that the whole time the Girl was sitting in a chair facing the blinding sun, the meeting was uneventful.

She didn't get a response or offer from Jake right away. She had to call him several times to follow up before he asked her to come to his office for a second interview. When she did come out to meet him again, as luck would have it, the only chair in front of his desk was the one facing the sun, so she was completely blinded yet again.

"I feel like I am being interrogated with the sun blinding me twice in a row. Have you planned it on purpose?" She joked.

"Of course," Jake smiled. "I wanted to see how well you can function under stress."

They chatted for a little bit longer and Jake did offer her a job. She was to start on May 2nd, which would give her two weeks after the tax season to rebound and reconnect with Max and the boys before diving into a new project.

***

As April was approaching, the office staff in the big open room at Walter Diggins started talking about the "life after tax season": how everyone was planning to celebrate the end of the season and what they were going to do for the rest of the year.

"What about you, Girl?" One of the coworkers asked.

"I will go skydiving after April 15," the Girl replied. She had made the decision to skydive when she got an offer from Jake. She needed something physical and powerful to move forward, so she thought jumping out of a plane would be the perfect solution.

"Skydiving? Are you serious?" Another coworker picked up on the conversation. "No way! Have you done it before?"

"Yes," the Girl did skydive once before, so she was familiar with the feeling she was chasing after. "In fact, the plane holds two people, so if there is anybody here who would want to keep me company on this adventure, please sign up. It will be cool to do it together!"

She didn't expect anyone to express interest, but a week later, the senior reviewer came up to her and started asking more questions. Ayisha was a fit mother of two, of Hindi descent, in her late 30s, and she was searching for an adrenaline boost. Skydiving filled that role just fine.

"Ayisha, if you and the Girl go together, I'll go with you," another mother of two boys said. "I'm not going to jump myself, but I just want to be there. *Seeing both of you jump will be enough for me.*"

For the next three weeks everyone in the open room had only one topic to discuss: the Girl's and Ayisha's skydiving. Some people did research on how safe it was, others expressed their opinions about being buckled up in a tandem way too close to a person they didn't know. This was a hot subject, and Ayisha seemed to be cool with it. She looked like a person who had made up her mind, and nothing would alter it.

On April 15 at the farewell company lunch, someone stirred the subject again. The Girl and Ayisha had already made a reservation to go out to a skydiving ranch a few days later, and everyone was curious.

"Walter," Chan started the conversation. "Did you know that the ladies are going skydiving in a few days?"

"No, I didn't." Walter replied. "Who's going?"

"Ayisha and Girl", someone else rejoined.

"Oh," he said understatedly. "I can imagine Girl doing it because she is so *wild,* but you, Ayisha? I would never expect that from you. Why in the world would you want to do something bizarre like that?"

Ayisha looked away and didn't answer. But the next day she called the Girl and asked her to cancel the reservation. She changed her mind and wasn't going to do it because she wasn't feeling well.

We don't lie to other people. We lie to ourselves while talking to other people.

Skydiving is one of the most powerful experiences a person can have during a dead-end period in life. It's far beyond an adrenaline rush. *Skydiving is a purposeful, self-imposed free fall jump in one direction, followed by a smooth scenic parachute ride that ends in a safe bumpy landing.* Resembles life, doesn't it? To the Girl, skydiving was a physical reboot of her internal computer, the awakening of herself within herself, a powerful force that was supposed to help her leave everything behind, including the rules, procedures, opinions, and conservative principles of Walter Diggins, in order to literally jump forward into the emptiness of the air, hopeful that the liberating flight would be pleasant, and the landing would be secure. In skydiving, there is no way back after the jump.

***

Freddie and Jake shared few similarities. Both were unpretentiously handsome, confident, witty men in their late 30's–early 40's. Both were slightly self-absorbed, but highly driven and talented in their professional arena. Both appreciated a comfortable lifestyle, fancy dining, and knew exactly what they wanted in business and how they were going to get it. In everything else, the men were poles apart.

Freddie was a creature of habit. His family came to the US 30 years ago, and since then had made great wealth by opening and maintaining a chain of high-end Persian restaurants in the best spots in the city. Freddie breathed luxury, designer brands, and lavish accessories. His office overlooked the ocean in one of the most prestigious beach districts, and while the office didn't look big or expensive, every item inside probably cost more than the Girl's quarterly salary. He specialized in the over-the-top multi-million dollar homes, and every person he met became an immediate friend, prospective client, or both. He had a wife and kids, loved to eat a lot of great food in extravagant restaurants, and shopped excessively for himself and his family.

"The first impression is the most important one," he would educate the Girl in a fatherly manner. "What brands you wear and how you present yourself matters – the clients have to see that you project success, denote business, and have the means to deliver the results."

Jake was a devoted yogi. The Girl didn't know

much about his background. All she knew was that he grew up on the East Coast, had few siblings, and loved to travel on his own. Outside of work, he was very reserved and preferred to spend time by himself. He enjoyed light gourmet food, unexplored places, and spa treatments. He cherished luxury hotels, but other than that he maintained a very low-key lifestyle. Jake was perfectly connected with himself and very much in touch with the world. His office dwelled on the 33rd floor in a downtown building with floor-to-ceiling windows, and he had scored the best view of the city skyline and the marina. When the Girl first walked into his office (for her second interview), she leaned to the window and gasped. It was a beautiful clear day and she could easily see the planes at eye level, preparing to land at the airport a few miles away; the water reflected the sun in a shiny and sparkly fashion; the parks, the people, and the buildings reminded her of a little toy game from childhood. "One day I will be at this level and all of this will be *my* view," she thought, trying to catch her breath, collect her thoughts, and come back to the reality of life without a job.

Freddie and Jake had very different work and management styles. Freddie was a micro-manager. Inflexible in his methods, he wanted to be involved in every aspect of the process. He had a hard time releasing the controls or exploring the possibilities. He only welcomed standardized employment; therefore the Girl had to be in the office every week for a designated number of hours, so he could *see* that the Girl was present and the work was being done. The lack of effectiveness of that arrangement in hi tiny office didn't make any difference to him. "I am 42 years old, I don't want to change my ways now," - he often repeated to her. Freddie had no problem bargaining for every penny just for fun. Even the smallest mistake would tailgate an hour-long pep-talk on the subject of what his dad did when he first came to this country, and built his first business without language or the knowledge of the domestic culture.

"If something goes wrong, it can't be my fault," he would say in conclusion of each pep-talk. "So either the CPA is to blame, or you." With that, Freddie had the biggest and the kindest heart and often reminded the Girl of a spring storm: quick to ignite and get angry, and just as quick to die down and move on.

Jake was open-minded and result-oriented. He was ready to spend as much money as needed to get the desired outcome. He welcomed virtual offices and telecommuting scenarios given that the job was done.

"You can be in Barcelona on the beach, for all I care, as long as you are plugged in and available," he declared to the Girl. With that, he expected everything to be triple-checked and confirmed. He would let a mistake slide the first time with a raised eye brow; however, the next time around the mistake was unforgivable. Jake was grounded and composed to such an extreme level that sometimes the Girl had a strong desire to shake him vigorously just to see if he was alive. He used the analytical and logical part of the brain to obtain the information he needed, but he always made decisions based on gut feeling. That stood for any kind of decision, including monetary.

The first time the Girl heard him say, "Hm, this profit doesn't feel right," she didn't believe her ears.

"What do you mean 'feel right'? This is pure math, numbers; you know, exact science!" She objected.

"Yeah," he agreed. "And something about this math doesn't feel right."

It took the Girl a while to get used to the concept of "feeling things" in business. Though she trusted her intuition on a personal level, she had never been exposed to this attitude in making financial or strategic decisions. Later on she would also learn from Jake to hire people based on the energy type required to complement or diversify the overall office energy, in order to keep the company balanced. For the longest time the Girl was obliged to retrain herself *to feel first and to think second* before she called Jake or entered his office. It wasn't an easy model to conceive, given how much it diverged from the mainstream approach which she had observed in her prior projects. But once she learned to accept this alternative business tactic, it became one of the most invaluable lessons she had ever learned in her early career.

Freddie was a savvy, established businessman, successful and persistent, the best of his kind. Though he preferred certainty in his personal dealings, he knew too well the first-handed pleasure of tricking any type of system. He went out of his way for his clients by exhausting every possible and available resource, disregarding the unnecessary limitations imposed by his brokerage firm in order to achieve the top results and an extraordinary level of satisfaction for his patrons. He used a "car salesman" style for his practice, but utilized it in the utmost unconventional and dynamic form, thus earning him nothing less than the absolute and deepest respect, in addition to well-deserved status as the top realtor in his area.

Jake was a strong, visionary leader, the kind that leads by example, by conviction, by unprecedented intelligence, and by the undeniable male energy of a fair warrior. He basically made you fall in love with his product by simply brushing his hands through the raw essence of it, with the contented self-assured look which left no doubts that he owned this product, he owned this company, and in a way he owned you for an instant of this conversation. Jake and Alex were two of the same breed. Men like them could not be contained in the framework of good or bad, smart or stupid, appropriate or not. They were so beyond standardized labeling, so much bigger and more complex on a deep psychological and personality level that it was practically impossible to fit them into these tiny boxes of social judgment and majority vote mentality. Therefore, they were often mistakenly perceived as intimidating and even offensive. They were totally intolerant of nonsense in a very indifferent, non-caring way. They didn't waste their time on things or people that didn't matter to them, and they didn't conceal it. As a result, they concentrated on what and who was actually meaningful in their lives. They led in a non-invasive, invitational way by their mere existence.

Next time your feminist girlfriend tells you that a woman needs to be number one in any relationship that involves men (including non-sexual relationships) and she should fight for equality with men at all times, don't believe her. She still has some growing up to do. *There is no greater feminine pleasure and honor for a strong, sophisticated, and self-sufficient woman than to be led by leaders like Jake and Alex and, yes, serve as the number two to them, by accepting the truth that they are the masters of their territory.* So instead of wrestling with them in their league games, you should give in to their masculine power, surrender into their protective energy and acknowledge your own territory which is, quite possibly, below theirs, but just as significant. True feminine power is neither about competing with fellow men for the prize of first place, nor is it about equal salaries, household duties, and the right to wear pants. It's about exploring, exploiting, and possessing what the Universe (or God) has given you and your kind thousands of years ago. So if you ever come across an opportunity to work alongside these men or to learn from them, be forever grateful for the gift of experiencing the true difference between strong male and female energies, the charity of the delight to be a number two to a sturdy leader, and the divine fulfillment of feeling what a true woman should feel: the joy of being led by generous and powerful men.

***

The projects were just as interesting and dissimilar as their owners.

Universal Distributions had been operated from the simplified and updated QuickBooks file and a basic spreadsheet. That setup was OK and the information was accurate; however, there was no structure to prepare the company for the promised growth in a multi-office scenario. Jake was interested in cloud options, new technologies, and cost-efficient, productive solutions. And whereas he always kept his finger on the financial pulse of the company, he wanted to be completely hands-off when it came to the day-to-day reporting operations, thus concentrating on sales, purchases, and relations development in order to sustain growth. He never limited the Girl in the amount and the type of research she could do, he only monitored the results and made sure that what was derived and implemented made sense for his vision of the company's future. In that, he often pushed the Girl to go back several times, research more, and think outside of the given context on practically every aspect of the company. He rarely ever disciplined the Girl on how she needed to proceed; he just let her be and do what she felt was needed, as long as he got a desirable outcome. He let her make her own mistakes and learn from them. The only times he would really lecture her would be when he reiterated over and over that he was building a fast-growing company, and if she ever had an issue with speed or the sweeping enthusiasm behind the growth, she should either change jobs or keep it to herself. The Girl never had an issue with this enthusiasm; in fact she admired and welcomed it. Jake made it easy for the Girl to stay true to herself, consequently establishing and maintaining infinite honesty and directness in their rapport. What resulted out of this open-ended work relationship, was a consummate QuickBooks Enterprise file with the Advanced Inventory add-on, backed by extensive but user-friendly spreadsheets and a completely cloud based (through Dropbox) filing system which allowed anyone within the company to have access to the appropriate files from anywhere in the world. The system was supported by the primitive, but documented written guidelines, and could be operated by the newly hired general staff by just following the instructions. This wasn't a perfect resolution by any definition, but it was a solid working model that was 85-90% functional in all required areas, easily upgradeable and interchangeable, bank and CPA audit-ready; but, most importantly, it allowed for a fast controlled takeoff, which was the ultimate goal of the whole process.

In Universal Distributions, the Girl had to be forward-thinking. But in Freddie's office, she was obliged to start with a backward path, before she could go forward. The fact that Freddie had changed so many bookkeepers within such a short period of time meant that there was complete chaos within his computer and paper files. In order to produce financials that were reasonable and accurate to the highest possible degree, the Girl had to go back and do a lot of reconstruction and forensic work. In addition, there had been no good record keeping for at least two years. To top all of this, Freddie had 10 different business accounts for personal reasons, and loved to juggle money back and forth from one account to the other, with multiple paper receipts to support the activity but no real tracking. The QuickBooks version was outdated, but Freddie resisted the upgrade for the longest time. Therefore all transactions had to be entered manually, which significantly slowed the progress of the project. When finally the initial cleanup was done, the Girl sighed with relief, hoping from that point on it would become easier. Then she realized there was more on her plate than she originally acknowledged. While Jake didn't even own a checkbook and all payments were made online after his review, Freddie liked to cut paper checks because he was used to that form of payment, and because it helped him with occasional tight cash flow. Besides, he was stubborn about releasing control of online banking. Therefore, all transactions had to be entered either manually or downloaded while he was present in the office. This was rare because he only made money while out showing properties and schmoozing with people, as any extraordinary realtor or salesman should. And though Freddie's project was considerably simpler in its magnitude, its execution was a pure game of patience, efficiency, and appreciation of old methods.

Both projects were challenging to the Girl in their own ways. But after a season of boring work at Walter Diggins office, her mind was so hungry to learn, grow, and absorb anything new that being challenged on both projects was robustly stimulating for her brain and fun for her soul. At that moment in her life, she wickedly enjoyed the fact that her brain was without rest, operating around the clock, looking for solutions, testing the unknown. Working on these projects simultaneously, switching back and forth from the peculiarities of one man to the other, reminded the Girl of the learning to write with both the right and the left hand at the same time.

Jake's approach seemed more intuitive to the Girl; Freddie's style was more explanatory. Freddie resembled Max in many ways (aside from his fascination with luxury, well-to-do family, and a few other minor details). Therefore, by unconditionally loving Max, it was simpler for the Girl to recognize what there was to love about Freddie: what his strong sides and distinguished quirks were. When something didn't make sense in Freddie's behavior, she often caught herself thinking what Max would do or how he would react in this case, and, most importantly, why he would act that way. Then everything immediately made sense. In the worst case scenario, she could always ask Max and he had no problem explaining the situations from his point of view.

With Jake, there was no one to ask but Jake himself. And though he was tremendously receptive and approachable, he demanded full commitment with no excuses.

"I want to be your number one priority, " he stated to the Girl one day during her second week on the job.

"I can't promise you that you will be the number one for me. What I can promise is that you, and Universal Distributions, will be placed on my list of important people, right *after* my husband, my kids, my parents, and my sister. Congratulations, you have just made it to the top five!" The girl responded, half-serious.

Jokes aside, the Girl knew precisely what was expected of her from Jake and Freddie. They were men before anything else, and they needed to know with a concrete certainty that when she was working for them, she was committed only to them. They both wanted to have exclusivity in her attention, skills, and efforts. The irony was in figuring out how to make these men a priority for her while that leading place was firmly and unquestionably occupied by Max, making him a distinctive number one in the Girl's life.

The rule says you are undeniably supposed to have a single number one person in your life, right? The reality shows though that you end up with several number one people, depending on where your life intersects with them (e.g. work, hobby, etc). So the real question is, how do you make several people (especially opinionated, weathered men, at least 10 years older), truly number one in your life without depriving each one of them of superiority in the field that belongs to them, and without spreading yourself too thin?

The Girl didn't have the answer to this intricate question. But instead of fiercely defending the rule of keeping only one number one person in her life (because if she supported that theory, she would inevitably end up without a job again), she decided to test the multiple number one option. Hence, she worked out a formula to be 120% committed solely to each of them: Max, Jake, or Freddie, when she was working on their "project," such that everyone felt special and significant in the way that was appropriate in that particular relationship. At home, she tried to turn off the phone at night and set at least few hours aside to spend with Max alone; in Jake's office she entirely shunned personal business; and with Freddie she put on hold all e-mails and messages from Jake and his team for the time being. This way, she found that she could sincerely concentrate on what was important at that moment in that particular place and at that particular time for that particular person: switching full focus, from one area to another, but not allowing herself to dilute her attention. The only exception to this scheme were emergencies in all departments. Did this setup always work flawlessly? Obviously, not. When something goes wrong, everything goes wrong. But at least it was a good start.

Not only was a full mental commitment required of the Girl for the projects, but also time, and availability, and dedication. Jake was dead serious when he made the statement that he didn't care where she was as long as she was plugged in and available. He meant it literally. The way this translated into the real world meant that she could be at home, in a coffee shop, on a plane, in a restaurant, or even taking a bath, but she needed to be "glued" to her laptop and cell-phone. Multiple times she caught herself pulling the car to the side curb when she was driving, taking out her laptop and answering immediate questions. Was it a healthy dependency? No. Was it optimally convenient? Not really. Was it an annoying trend? Very much so. Was it better than the structured 9am-to-5pm office schedule? The Girl couldn't answer that one.

For the majority of the population, structure is better, because at the very least, one can leave work at work at the end of the day, and can go home to family and forget about employment-related issues until the next morning. There is an immense certainty that tomorrow is going to resemble yesterday. As a price for the luxury of an empty-headed evening, these people were bound to the office regime of set hours, even though they (much like the Girl) weren't exactly their most productive selves all the time. The Girl never knew or understood the beauty of the not-taking-work-home frame of mind. She could in no way control her mind; she couldn't stop continuous analysis at a certain hour while occupied with an engaging project. Her mind would light up with excitement, like the snap of fingers, when it was in a "hibernate mode" due to dullness of the tasks on hand. With the flexibility provided by Universal Distributions, the Girl could take breaks, go out in the middle of the day, take care of her personal issues and kids during normal work hours, and come back to finish the workload at night time, when she was refreshed. On the flip side, she was hooked 24/7. Nevertheless, all logical arguments paled in comparison with what this flexibility gave her on the inner level, but she couldn't pinpoint or define that feeling…until several months later.

In July, the Girl and Max took a week-long vacation to the East Coast for their self-imposed "college tour," as they jokingly called it. They planned to visit Harvard and Princeton, but even more so they wanted to explore Boston and New York in depth. During this time, the Girl was supposed to work at her usual flexible schedule. One day she needed to process some invoices. She clearly imprinted that day in her memory because it gave her a new meaning, a new understanding of where she was, and even showed a tiny unrecognizable glimpse of where she wanted to be in the future.

It was around 1pm in the afternoon. Max and the

Girl were resting on a bench in the park in the very center of Boston on a perfectly beautiful summer day, a little tired after wandering around the city, eating the best salmon burgers they had ever tried, and sipping a glass of chilled white wine. And on that bench, with the laptop in her hands and Max by her side peacefully reading his book, she looked at the gorgeous view of the city, inhaled the unfamiliar air of the American European Boston, and thought to herself: *this is what conditional freedom feels like. You can be yourself and enjoy your life the way you want, but on someone else's terms.* To the Girl, this conditional freedom was by far the most liberating solution within the scope of her knowledge, much superior to the cluttered and controlled office environment, and despite certain inconveniences, she definitely appreciated it a great deal more.

4

THE BIRTH OF BOOXKEEPING

Max and the Girl have just celebrated their 10 year anniversary. Their characters were complete opposites, but they shared the same priorities and have developed common interests over time. Where the Girl's amplitude of feelings and experiences was overly expressive and often oscillated between the extreme highs and lows, Max was a lot more level-headed and reasonable. He was the epitome of a family man, authentic protector, who divided all people in two categories: close circle and everyone else. While he would go out of his ways for loved ones in his close circle, he wouldn't lift a finger for anyone else. "I have limited energy, and I choose to spend it on people who really matter to me", he would often say to the Girl. The Girl loved in a very romantic, unprecedented, but forgiving and tolerant way, similar to the device operated on batteries; Max loved statically, in an unwavering and equally charged manner, like a device that was constantly plugged to an electrical outlet. He was extremely well-rounded and knowledgeable. The amount of active information in his head—the quotes, the dates, the facts, the books, the political leaders and their parties, the historical events—have always been a source of endless admiration for the Girl. Max had an enormous heart and care for people. Not only did he remember their names, occupations, diseases, businesses, miscellaneous affiliations and interests, and their kids' and dogs' names, but he really sincerely cared about what was going on in their lives at any given point. On the flip side, he only gave one chance. Earning a second chance was the hard and almost impossible thing to do. Moreover, he was very artistic in a theatrical kind of way, and had an incredible, light and witty sense of humor that immediately attracted people to him. *Max's power was magnificent in its steadiness, reminiscent of that of a titan who was able to run the whole world for you with the easiness of a feather, while holding your torso with such a strong unconditional love that it lifted you above the world, allowing you to see the unseen and to feel the unfelt.*

Max and the Girl were one of those eccentrically cute, romantically teasing , unpredictably amusing, and unexpectedly deep couples. Once you met them, you a hard time forgetting them, whether you liked them or not. They were true partners in everything they owned, being equally comfortable and exuberant in visiting a synagogue or a strip club together, dancing or day-dreaming, working long hours or getting lost during a night on the town, jumping through the roof with excitement or curling into a corner upset. They went through the necessary share of sharp ups and downs in their mutual life and figured out their differences and roles with each other a long time ago. And though they did still occasionally fight like many other couples, every night they went to sleep together, come hell or high water, thus reconciling any unresolved matters by the morning. Each one was a whole in his or her own way, yet together they oddly completed each other.

Max knew that the Girl wasn't thrilled with the contracts. Though her mind was challenged, her creative fuels were untapped. So to keep the Girl happy and animated, and to add variety to their otherwise routine-driven lives, he would hijack the Girl and take her on short, one-to-two day staycation trips up north to Orange County and Los Angeles to see friends, enjoy shows, or just hang out by the beach. The Girl loved those trips with Max, where it was just the two of them being their playful and adventurous selves. They could converse or stay silent and absent-minded with equal pleasure.

On one of those trips, the Girl has shared with Max the vision that had been haunting her ever since the tax season at Walter Diggins office. The vision included a unique bookkeeping company that operated by 21st century standards, utilizing cloud and technology-based solution to the utmost potential, and serving small-to-midsized business with a "what else can we do for you" customer service approach. The key was that this company would focus strictly on one special aspect of accounting—bookkeeping—but contain all-inclusive services within that field. Max loved the idea. He had a finance background as well and did some bookkeeping contracts on the side while he was in school, so he could totally relate. Since then, on every trip they would discuss the concept over and over again, but nothing original or inventive would come of it.

One late spring night Max and the Girl were sitting

in a hip bar, sipping iced water. They came for a close friend's birthday party, but both were on Penicillin prescriptions due to a case of strep throat, so they couldn't consume any alcohol – usually the express purpose of hitting the bar. They also didn't know anybody in their friend's crowd. So they were stuck for several hours watching the Los Angeles hipsters and fashionistas, but also playing "what if" scenarios for the new unnamed business venture. And then, all of a sudden, the Universe (God???) opened its doors and everything just clicked. The whole concept flashed in front of their eyes: the services, the employee perks, the business, the operational structure, the pricing model, etc. They bounced ideas back and forth, like a ping pong ball, and every idea evolved into something beautiful and distinctive.

The name came a little later. On some other trip (yes, Max and the Girl made a lot of important decisions during their trips), they were talking about the business again, playing with words and word connections, and all of a sudden the Girl remembered the book she read (and never finished) about a year before. It was a business/personal journal of the New York restaurateur Danny Meyer's, called *Setting the Table: the Transforming Power of Hospitality in Business*. While some books are fountainheads of knowledge, others are books of one statement. To the Girl, Danny Meyer's book was the latter. He described how he was looking for a name for his Union Square Café restaurant, playing with words and concepts (kind of like Max and the Girl were doing), and his mentor said to him: "Call it what it is." Ever since then, this phrase was an internal joke between the Girl and Max when they were regarding to someone acting up, but not admitting it. But in this particular case the expression was, in fact, completely appropriate.

"Call it what it is," she quoted the book to Max. "BooXkeeping, bookkeeping with a twist."

They came back home, registered the name and the website, created a logo and wrote the content for the website. Thus, BooXkeeping was born.

***

Trial and error is the most effective method of learning because it's active; it literally requires taking action in order to make mistakes before you start learning from them. And the sooner you start making those mistakes, the faster you will learn.

Max and the Girl came to the conclusion that Max would take care of the business development and front end part of the business. His service business finally became sustainable on its own to the point where he didn't need to participate in it full-time, so he had spare time, as well as the desire, to pursue this opportunity. The girl was still highly involved with Universal Distributions and Freddie's practice, so she was limited on the time aspect. Besides, she would much rather stay "behind the scenes"; it was more in her character, and her expertise was a lot more technical. According to their agreement, she would be building operations and performing the work until they hired somebody, as well as participating in the technical part of the sale.

Establishing a new business is very much like raising a newborn. The first year is the toughest: the

0-3 months are impossible, 3-6 months are unclear and exhausting, 6-9 months are challenging, and 9-12 months are a lot of work.

You've been fantasizing about this baby for the longest time, but as soon as you bring home the hungry and screaming charmer, you have absolutely no clue what to do with him. Everyone says that the motherly instinct comes naturally right away, and you are patiently waiting for it to magically appear and guide you, but it just... doesn't. Your motherly instinct is nowhere to be found. About three months later you realize that the miracle has actually already happened... at the point when the baby was born... and there is no additional magic to be expected any time soon. That's when it hits you that raising a baby will be work (not that you didn't know about it, or no one warned you): hard work that inevitably involves a lot of mistakes, some of which might be potentially dangerous—but there is just no other way to learn how to connect with this baby and how to provide to him all that he needs, other than to keep making those mistakes and learning from them. This realization changes your prospective towards the parenting process. So you stop relying on a conceptual motherly instinct and start involving active research (books, videos, forums, other mothers, grandparents, etc.). At this stage, you are bound to the information overload because all of a sudden everyone seems to know how to raise your baby. And though some people actually share words of wisdom, others are just as clueless as you are, but they don't want to admit it. Instead of being objective or abstaining from offering advice, they assure you that it's hard for everybody (like that statement seriously ever helps!). This is where you start to learn how to listen to yourself and your baby by trying and failing, trying and getting no results, trying and succeeding, thus *developing motherly instinct. Motherly instinct is a crossover between internal love and external experiences; it is not given, rather it is a process in the making.*

When you make it through the first year, you feel an eternity older, but this is essentially only the beginning. Somewhere along the line of the first year you have perhaps also learned to enjoy the baby despite the inconveniences and hardships, and with every following year, as you keep mastering the skills and expanding your love, you deepen and improve your connection with this child. It's also at this point when you decide for yourself how much involvement you want to have with this baby: is it going to be a 24/7 dependency, or a balanced relationship where you get to do what you love for some time by releasing control (to the babysitter), but then you also spend quality time with this child. This decision eventually translates in the eminence of your life with this baby, which everyone surely chooses for himself.

Do you see the similarities between business development and baby raising? How many times have you heard from others that you will be just "natural" as a businesswoman or businessman and you will have no problems whatsoever accomplishing anything, only to realize as soon as you roll on your own that there is nothing natural about this process other than the pure game of mistakes and resolutions, which ultimately leads to practical experiences? How different is the *business instinct from the motherly instinct?* Maybe someone should collaborate with Heidi Murkoff, the author of *What to Expect when You are Expecting,* and *What to Expect the First Year* (by the way, the most intelligible books on parenting that exist out there today) and compile business versions of her books. Could be bestsellers too, who knows.

For Max and the Girl, BooXkeeping wasn't their first business. But just like with children, though everything seems easier with the second child simply because you have made the initial batch of parenting mistakes and now, at least, you know what to expect, different children require different approaches. So do different businesses.

The biggest challenge for the couple lay in finding the first group of new clients. Their days were filled with networking breakfasts, lunches, meetings, coffees, dinners, and happy hours. Max and the Girl would experiment with door-to-door marketing, walking from one small business to another; they joined several chambers of commerce, and informed everyone they met on what they were doing. They executed a lot of pro-bona work to get a foot in the door. They tried cold calling or mass e-mailing. Some people would comment that the accounting and bookkeeping market was oversaturated and there were no opportunities available. Others were very discouraging when they mentioned how difficult times were due to the recession, and how it was almost impossible to find any business out there, because they tried and they couldn't.

The Girl had heard the same lines about nine months prior, when she was looking for a job. This common outlook, the "nothing is available" mentality, reminded her a lot of the *women's bathroom effect: everyone is obediently waiting in line (with some women who are in a desperate need to go) assuming that if people in front of them were already in line, they have confirmed that all cabins are taken. If you proceed forward to look under the stalls or simply go and knock every closed door, you are being judged as strange and rude. However, statistically, there is at least a 30% chance that you will find an empty stall, an opportunity waiting just for you, in a full bathroom with a line of people. You may be wasting time, but if you catch the unoccupied stall, it's fully yours to use right away.* Some people prefer to stand in lines their whole life because it is a socially acceptable model of behavior. Other individuals, like the Girl and Max, take their chances and search for empty stalls, even if others look down at them.

At that time, their office was located in an open tiny loft inside their house. The loft fit one large table and a few filing cabinets, had no doors, no interior walls, and no sound-proofing. Their youngest son was still at home with a babysitter and had great fun being himself: a loud, willful, excited, and hyperactive 18-22 month old boy who would occasionally play hide-and-seek, searching for his mom, who was desperately trying to get something done in this madness. Therefore to accommodate the work, especially the conference calls, the Girl had to occasionally find the quietest place in the house, which ended up being a tiny walk-in closet behind the master bedroom. She would take her laptop and cell phone with a set of headphones, lock all doors that led to the closet, and thus disappear in this little black hole, sitting on the floor for hours trying to stay focused on a call or a task. Jake particularly was a heavy user of conference calls. That had always been an enormous challenge to the Girl, since she was a very visual and kinesthetic perceiver but totally did not collect information audibly, so any phone conversation required a double effort. Every time Max came home and found her still working there, he would scream through the locked doors, chuckling.

"The Girl, don't you think it's time for you to come out of the closet?"

Their spending marketing budget equaled zero. Max and the Girl had finally started to climb out of the debts they had incurred in the past year, and between the income from the Girl's contracts and Max's service business, they were barely making it through their monthly overhead expenditures. The only resources for business development that they really had were their minds, their bodies, their experiences, and several friends in different industries who were ready to do favors for them. They had to stay creative within their means. One time in early September, in search of new clients, they decided to participate in a Chamber of Commerce trade show. They had $130 to spend on a booth. So they rented a white background ($80), a small contemporary white stand for the flyers ($10), printed a sign($25), and bought the simplest tripod ($15). They hung the white background over the standard black or blue pipe-and-drape provided with a space, stationed a tripod with the logo in the center, and put a stand with flyers in the corner. The logo was black and red on white background, so it coordinated well with the rest of the completely white arrangement. This way, they created a photo-shoot like environment where the center of attention was not a model, but... a logo, or essentially a company. Tradeshow visitors continuously complimented them on how clean, simple, and unexpected this setup was within the environment of that tradeshow. But so were their services; therefore the concept fit to the t. Max and the Girl did end up with a few leads from the tradeshow which evolved into new clients about six months later.

Nothing boosts the imagination like a lack of money.

Max and the Girl were spending time together but one could hardly call it quality time. They were running around trying to juggle all activities, their service and BooXkeeping businesses, contracts, kids, and occasional outings. The biggest difficulty was to stay alert and on top of the activity they were engaged in at the moment. One particular Friday in mid-fall served as a quintessential example of what it was like to be them during this period: the mix of unmixable activities that together are called living.

The day was planned with back-to-back activities. In the morning, the Girl had to take care of some invoices, payments, and reports for Universal Distributions. Right after, they rushed to a funeral and memorial service for a close friend of the family — the sad but harshly realistic reminder of how short and precious life is. Later, they visited one of the properties for Max's business, where he needed to walk around with a property manager and give him an estimate on services. Then, they headed to a resort located on the other side of the city, where the Girl needed to drop of a flower arrangement for an auction (she still wasn't ready to give up the event design world). After that, they headed to a CPA connection mixer in order to find some referral sources for new clients. Then, they had a quick dinner on the fly, only to rush to the theater for a play. Theater was by far one of their biggest mutual passions. However on that night, by the time they sat down to enjoy the performance, their day felt completely surreal. They weren't able to make out who they were, what they were, or what really mattered on the grander scale . Their reality was faintly blurred.

***

During the same period, the Girl was endlessly searching for ways to bring creativity into accounting without jeopardizing the financial results. In her mind and her world, to be creative meant to dream; to dream meant to live. So ultimately, by transitive law, the Girl was looking for an opportunity to bring life into the dull, colorless science of accounting, and primary associations related with the people who chose this profession.

One of the ideas she tested was to simplify dress code when meeting with clients, in order to correlate with the colors of the logo, thus subconsciously promoting the business. So she and Max decided they would only wear black, grey or white clothing (with occasional red accessories for her in the form of bracelets, scarves etc). The concept was great in theory; however, when she looked inside her closet four months later, she was blown away by how prematurely boring it looked. She was only 27, loved bright colors, and wasn't ready to commit suicide because of the depression caused by the colors of her logo. So that idea was a fail.

Another idea she tested had to do with self introduction at breakfast networking events. She became a part of a small network group through yet another organization. The group met every Thursday. In the beginning of each meeting before the presentation, each member of the group had 40 seconds to introduce himself. As a standard, people would say their names, what they did, and a little bit about their businesses. Sounds perfect, right? Well, the Girl didn't think so. It was indeed a great idea for the first or second introduction. But when she saw the same people every week for several months in a row, she could repeat each of their lines in her sleep. That deprived her of the intrigue of what new information she was going to learn on that particular meeting about the people she was mingling with. If she were to talk about bookkeeping every week for 40 seconds, the subject would bore everyone to death. So she decided to diverge from the standard introduction. Instead, every week she would come up with a current and ongoing fact from the fields she loved (travel, theater, book quotes, new restaurants or experiences), but at the end of every introduction she would divert the message back to the core of her business, MasterCard style. She would often finish in this manner: "Go on. Go out. Spend time with your family. Outsource your bookkeeping." Was that a good idea? It was original. Initially there was a serious rejection of her method; however, within a month, people started to expect that they would learn something new every time she introduced herself. If she occasionally did talk about bookkeeping, they actually became noticeably upset. One thing was for sure: the people at the table remembered her. But even more important, she was now introducing herself in her own way, in a way that let her stay true to herself.

She did quit that networking circle about seven months later. She was getting some leads through the group; however, the time and effort that she invested in order to attend the breakfast every week at 7 am wasn't worth the type or amount of work she received from those leads. But the concept of sharing messages and news about a variety of mind-engaging subjects within the context of bookkeeping and numbers became the beginning for what would evolve into a weekly company newsletter about a year later.

The one who is afraid of experiments will never learn the essence of originality.

***

Whatever directions the Girl and Max took, whatever methods they tried, whatever service modifications they offered, whoever they met, they still didn't seem to hit upon a recipe for how to get clients. They got leads, but all leads were fairly raw and yielded no results at that point. Until that day, the only BooXkeeping client they really had was

Freddie.

The couple was disappointed. They never expected a quick turn out or the easy road, nor did they hope in a delusional way that once they created the company, thousands of customers would run screaming and fighting to use their services, thus making them instant millionaires. They knew better than that due to prior failures.

What bothered them was that for the last six months they had dedicated themselves to exploring any route that could lead to a potential client—yet so far there was no feedback. It felt like they were throwing their efforts into the Universe (to the God), but it was taking its sweet time to get back to them. It wasn't until Christmas that they got *the phone call.*

The couple originally planned to spend the Christmas in Las Vegas. A friend from overseas was supposed to come for the holidays, and they were hoping that they could use this vacation as downtime to spend with their kids and their friend, since there was zero activity in the BooXkeeping business, and there was a slowdown within their service business and Jake's contract. But as destiny would have it, everything turned upside down within two days. Their friend flew in from overseas, but he had to turn around and go back home within 48 hours to take care of an emergency. As a result, the Vegas trip was cancelled, and the couple stayed home for Christmas.

The call came in on Christmas Day from one of the enrolled agents that they have been trying to connect with for a few months. Her client needed to close out two years worth of bookkeeping in order to file taxes, but he actually had shoeboxes full of stuff and she needed someone to complete the project within two weeks. This meant there would be no downtime for the holidays. The project was convoluted, and the Girl needed to start working on it right away. It also meant the Universe (with or without God) had finally responded.

5

BEWARE OF THE CLIENTS

The first project is always the most memorable. It's also most often the worst imaginable project. The client, which was a small dealership that sold used cars, consisted of a rare combination (the most fun kind that exists out there for a bookkeeper): the boxes of receipts and check registers were supposed to be exchanged for program-generated intelligent statements, and the owner didn't have the time or desire to answer any questions until his accountant called him three times with a reminder to file the tax return extension.

Of course, Max and the Girl didn't make any profit on their first client. They were desperate for any customer to get the ball rolling, so they gave a proposal cheap enough to get the project. They needed an action that would activate the chain reaction, which would ultimately result in quality clients.

The same enrolled agent sent another client with the same request a few weeks later. This time it was a technology company, which was 3 years old, and had never filed a tax return. The project was of the same magnitude and complexity. But at least it was a second real BooXkeeping client, which fit the model, the services, and the business concept. When the couple received a check from this client, their profit amounted to $400, so they went out to a fancy restaurant to celebrate. Max had cashed the deposit check, but the money fell out of his pocket while he was smoking a cigar on the balcony, and was immediately stolen. Though they earned the money on this project, they didn't see any of it.

Then there was another CPA who needed the books closed for a client. All of a sudden, the projects started to roll in out of nowhere, one by one: via referrals, contacts, networking. It was the beginning of the calendar year, the era of new resolutions, and many small business owners made a New Year's Resolution to have a smooth bookkeeping process and a clean set of books completed on time. On the other hand, it was a tax preparation season, and many CPA's, as well as their clients, didn't have the time or resources to complete all preparation work, so they were only too happy to outsource it. Most projects were for-profit; however, there was a peculiar trend in the couple's financial situation: as soon as they started making a little more money than what was needed beyond their bare minimum household expenses, something unexpected, like a broken car, root canals for their son, or anything else of that sort would happen, thus bringing them back to square one and wickedly ruling out the financial incentive of the business development process. It was like they had an undetectable financial ceiling, and they couldn't break through it until they learned something radically important, something that would take them to a new level—not only financially, but professionally and personally.

There was finally progress in the BooXkeeping development: slow but visible progress. All projects were a mess; all were challenging and with constraints; all consisted of some kind of issue waiting to be resolved before the job could be completed. The Girl spent a lot of time making mental notes on every process that she was involved with. She needed to find a unified model, an approach that would help her come into any client's business despite the industry and size, and let her quickly assess what needed to be done, how it was going to be completed, within what timeframe, and at what cost. The more inclusive and structured the approach was going to be, the more effective she (and eventually her employees) could be with clients. She went back to Universal Distributions and Freddie's projects, and reevaluated what work she had really done, and, most importantly, how it was done. She then went even further back in her memory to the times when she was only starting in the field of accounting, and to her first few controller jobs, and did the same. She also raided her event planning experiences for any patterns. After a long and intensive analysis, she found a trend in how she approached any project; but the most fascinating part of that discovery was that the same trend represented a formula, a key to the way she lived her own life.

First and foremost, the Girl always walked into a client's office with a firm determination to start the meeting with a clean slate. When you are invited into somebody's world, it is crucial to leave your beliefs and opinions outside. She realized all too well from her personal experience how flawed a first impression could be. She was often misread herself by other people, and she knew deep in her heart how it felt to be judged, to be condemned, to be misunderstood. Being non-judgmental was an easy and a completely natural undertaking for her. She accepted human beings for who they were: *strong multifaceted characters that were perfect in their imperfections*. It didn't mean that she liked everybody. What it did mean was that she could find positive and negative traits in any person she dealt with, and to the Girl, the existence of both sides was normal. It was OK to be brilliant in one field and completely ludicrous in another; to her, there was nothing wrong with this blend. Most small business owners at the very least deserved great respect for the simple fact that they had the guts to go out on their own and let go of the comforts of a corporate life. The last thing they needed was to have someone come and tell them how to run their world. They were looking for support, not leadership — for one specific task, intelligently finished and closed. Bookkeeping was a supporting task, and one of the top five tasks ranked by significance to the vitality of a business. The Girl always made sure that she came with an open mind to complete this task.

Next, the Girl spent a great deal of time evaluating the current *reality* of a client's situation. What was the current situation? What were the pitfalls? What worked and what didn't? What was acceptable and satisfactory and what needed to be changed? *Clear, honest assessment of a reality helps to define the starting point, which is a fundamental initial step for the success of a process.* If you don't know where you started, how can you estimate progress? She glanced over the financials of accounting clients with a critical eye, and asked numerous questions about the business processes and responsibilities and task allocation within the company, thus identifying problem areas that had an impact on the bookkeeping. With event design clients, she inquired about the specifics of what the event was, what had already been planned and was going fine, and what areas the clients really needed help with. She demanded to know top three priority items for the clients, because she accepted that people are different in what matters to them, and this helped her to confine the client's reality into a tangible format.

Then, the Girl worked with the other party on establishing a *vision* for a project. *Vision sets the destination for a project and is an ending point of the process.* Just like with navigation systems, in order to go anywhere and start the route, you need the beginning and the ending point. The vision doesn't always have to be precise; the approximate vision will still provide the direction for the process. This concept was a lot easier perceived with event planning clients. After she obtained all the details for the needs and current situations of her clients, she always called for them to close their eyes and then she asked: "Now if the budget wasn't an issue and anything was possible, what would you want your event to be? What would it look, feel, smell, and sound like?" As soon as she started getting answers, she would push the clients even further, in David Tutera style: "Dream Bigger." All she was really doing was taking her clients out of the comfort zone of replicating somebody else's celebration and pushing them to dream on their own, thus bringing their true DNA into their own event and making it a continuous expression of themselves. With accounting clients, the task of defining a vision was far more complicated for the simple reason that somehow business owners didn't ever put the words "vision" and "bookkeeping" together in their minds, let alone "dream" and "bookkeeping," so they often looked at her at first like she was a psychopath. She knew exactly why she needed to figure out their vision for a project, so their initial reaction never bothered her. However, the communication of the purpose of this task to the customer was still a huge challenge. Her real advantage lay in the fact that most of the time, the owners were in such a crisis within their accounting or bookkeeping department, that they were ready to do anything to have it resolved. So they just gave in to this odd young woman, and thus she had it her way (for the future benefit of the clients). Whatever it takes to get results.

When the Girl identified the starting and the ending points of the project (the reality and the vision), she was ready to work on the most involved and the least defined practice of creating a flexible route: indicating the methods, the procedures, the timeframes, and the milestones. Afterward, she proceeded with the voyage from the reality to the vision via the changes, adaptations, occasional mistakes, corrections, and new lessons learned. While the beginning and the ending points of this journey were very clear to the client, the course itself was most often outside of their expertise, and therefore a complete mystery.

Somewhere in the middle of the process, when you are almost equally far from the reality and the vision in such a way that you lose the sight of both, comes a <u>Circle of Blindness</u> which is accompanied by frustration, distrust, and resentment. This is the hardest part of the process, that is also unavoidable. Many people give up when they hit the Circle of Blindness and come back to where they started. Also, many visions are being reevaluated at this stage, which refines the future process. The Girl found that working through the Circle of Blindness with her clients involved a lot of patience, hand-holding, and reaffirmation that a structured approach to the issue indeed existed. She had to convince clients that this part of the process was nothing but a temporary, inevitable inconvenience. She didn't like this part of the process either. Her clients were unhappy and felt lost; therefore, they endlessly questioned the validity of the whole concept, as well as her skill set, and even tried to take control. At this stage she conditioned herself to stay grateful to her clients for their trust, because in this scenario she was playing the role of the "legally blind" guide in the dining-in-the-dark experience.

The process eventually resulted in a *new reality: a hybrid between the initial reality and the initial vision, on a new level.* Sometimes the new reality would hit the vision on the head (in this case, the original vision was a quantifiable goal), or would represent a revised concrete version of the initial vision (here the original vision was a dream, which is always elusive in its form).

The Girl called this process the <u>ReVision Triangle</u>

approach.

*The ReVision Triangle is a shifting process from the existing **RE**ality to the **VISION** through a series of revisions in the character, skill set and frame of mind of the individual or the entity, thus resulting in a new reality. In mathematical relationship form, the formula is* $R \rightarrow V = R_1$ (Exhibit 1).

The continuous growth is an infinite one-way flow from one ReVision Triangle to the next, where new reality becomes a starting point for the next ReVision Triangle; hence it requires a new vision, and eventually results in the next reality. $R \rightarrow V = R_1 \rightarrow V_1 = R_2$ (Exhibit 2).

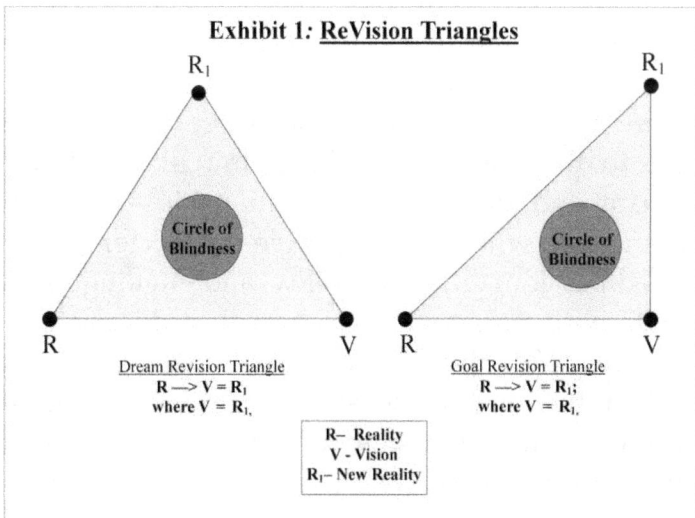

Exhibit 1: ReVision Triangles

R_1 R_1

Circle of Blindness   Circle of Blindness

R   V   R   V

Dream Revision Triangle   Goal Revision Triangle
$R \rightarrow V = R_1$ $R \rightarrow V = R_1$;
where $V = R_1$,   where $V = R_1$,

R– Reality
V - Vision
R_1– New Reality

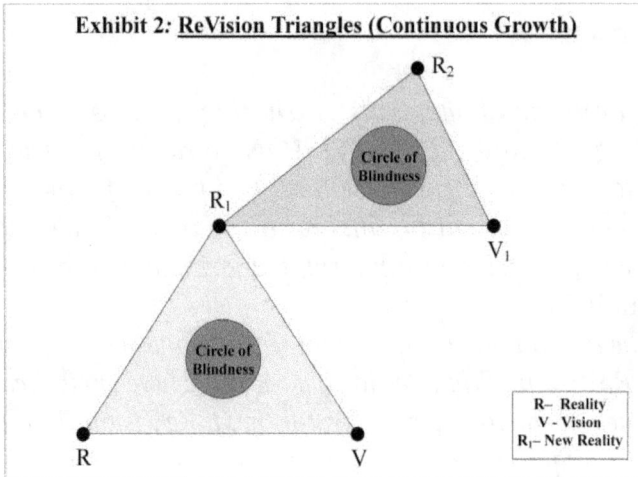

Exhibit 2: ReVision Triangles (Continuous Growth)

The Girl derived the module from experiences with her clients. However, she quickly tested it and recognized that the same formula prevailed in her private life. For example, about three years ago she came to the reality that she didn't like to have a stagnant and dull married relationship—living like roommates—which many people settled for (R); she needed passion, unpredictability, and ongoing mental growth with a man who was a partner, a lover, and a best friend (V). In the process of developing their bond at the next level, she and Max split up for several months and were on the verge of divorce (Circle of Blindness). They went through a long series of adjustments in their beliefs and characters before their relationship evolved into what it was now (R1).

It also didn't take her long to recognize what was currently happening to her. A year ago, the Girl had no money or sustainable source of income for the family (R). She had craved running her own business, where she could stay creative, productive, flexible, and make a profit, while continuously stimulating her mind (V). Right now she was working her way through that particular ReVision Triangle, and only God (or the Universe) knew where it would lead her; what the new reality would be.

The module proved to be universal. It fit in both professional and personal worlds.

***

In the beginning of January, the Girl received a phone call from a manager in the Walter Diggins office. The manager was inquiring about whether she was interested in working another tax season for them. The girl needed money, though not as desperate as the year before, and she agreed to do it on conditional terms. She now had other time commitments between Universal Distributions, Freddie's real estate office, and her own early clients, which she wasn't planning to give up, because unlike Walter Diggins opportunity, these arrangements were sources of income throughout the year. She could only offer herself to work two full days a week on Fridays and Saturdays. Last year she wasn't allowed to work full-day Saturdays because there was barely anybody in the office and there was limited supervision. Another issue was with her desk in the office. Since April, Walter Diggins had hired two more junior staff members. All desks in the open room were taken, so the Girl offered to set up a desk in the storage room and work out of there. The storage room was a quiet filing place in the furthest corner of the office, which due to its location permitted a distinctive lack of control. Last year, on particularly loud and busy days, she would ask to use the desk in that unutilized space to be able to concentrate better, but this request was denied along with many others. The manager jotted down her terms and said she would call her back, though she honestly didn't think that Walter would agree to any of it. Neither did the Girl.

Why did she insist on those terms? Mostly, she needed this setup to keep her clients and to run her own business on her cell phone by replying to frequent phone calls and writing e-mails, or to login remotely to her home computer without many eyes looking over her shoulder. But there was also a pinch of rebel in that request. Last year, she could have zero flexibility no matter how much she asked, so she was just testing the waters for the hell of it.

To her surprise, Walter called her back himself in a few days and was extremely sweet and apologetic, saying he was totally fine with all of her requests and he was just very sorry for the inconvenience it would cause her since he couldn't come up with a better, more socially appropriate seating arrangement for her for the next two and a half months. "Inconvenience? Are you kidding me?" She thought to herself in happy disbelief. Without knowing it, Walter was doing her the biggest favor of all time. She could use the best of both worlds: come, learn, and make money in an extremely structured office, and mentally disappear while being highly productive in her own way without unnecessary supervision. Since she was a part-timer, she didn't need to go through the routine boring meetings, yearly reviews, and unneeded procedures, and that was a huge perk in itself. And more importantly, she had finally found a way to work in the CPA office while staying entirely true to herself and her own work ethics: something she previously thought was absolutely unfeasible the way she was wired.

The Girl had been out of touch with the Walter Diggins office staff since April 15, so there was a lot to catch up on.

"Did you jump last year?" Everyone was asking her as soon as she strolled into the office.

"Yes, I did. " She responded in a matter-of-fact way.

"Really? How was it? How did it feel? Are you going to jump again this year?"

She couldn't grasp this heightened interest in such a small and private matter as skydiving. It felt almost like they were searching for the frantic confirmation that at least someone *did it*, that it was possible and real. It also felt like by jumping herself, she somehow was able to jump for all of them, for each and every one of them. The Girl couldn't explain this feeling, but deep in her core she felt it's intense pressure.

Another favorite, and the most touched-upon subject, was her desk arrangement.

"Have you seen where they put you?" Everyone mentioned with an interest.

"Yeah, I did." She answered in the same manner in which she addressed the questions about skydiving. "In fact, it was my idea, and I love every inch of it."

"Really? I would never want to be shoved in the corner like *this* all by myself. It's embarrassing and inappropriate! Are you crazy?" Was a common comment.

This comment consistently brought the Girl back to the article that she came across in the *Rental Units Magazine* a while back. The article was about new emerging trends in services offered to property management companies, apartment complexes, and homeowner's associations. The first sentence of the article unexpectedly declared: *"I am not crazy. I am just not you."*

Ironically, as much as everyone in the office was hypercritical of her desk in the storage room, she was the only one, besides the managers and Walter, who had what resembled a private office, unlike the rest of the staff in the open room. And as the busy season unfolded, what was an "inappropriate" arrangement a month ago became the hottest seat in the house.

"I envy you," The same reviewer who wanted to watch her and Ayisha skydive said, while searching for files in the storage room. "You get to sit in the most peaceful place in the whole office and actually get work done, while we are bound to limited concentration with all this talking and phone conferencing in the open room."

"You can have my spot for the four days of the week that I'm not here. I can rent it by the hour." The Girl giggled in response.

The Girl could not stop wondering about the reasoning behind the idiosyncrasies of the hierarchical environment, like the one she witnessed in Walter Diggins office. The only difference in her physical status in the office compared to the last year was that last year she was the youngest person in the office, and the latest hire. This year, she was neither. But why were these little things, these insignificant attributes of ranking, so imperative? Why last year, when she completed her first two or three projects way ahead of her budgeted hours, she was called in Walters' office, and instead of receiving a pat on the back, she got an ear full about how fast she worked, and how *she needed to slow down to blend in with the rest?* But this year, when she looked at her task list for the season, she had about 80 percent of her last year's list while she could only work 40 percent of the time, which implied that it was OK now, it was almost expected that she work at her natural speed. Where was the consistency behind this logic? Or why did every accountant have to spend about 30 minutes per project to fix the margins on the completed financial statements, when realistically each one of them could whip up an additional tax return during the same time frame, while a receptionist, who was paid time and a half less than the average accountant, could totally cope with on her own? Why last year, when she had a few free hours and she offered the secretary to help with labeling and stamping envelopes for tax planning, had she gotten a few dirty looks, like she brought shame to the clan of the accountants because she chose to do such a basic undervalued task, when *it wasn't her job?* In no way was she judging the methodology of this business structure. On the contrary, she was very grateful to Walter yet again, but this time it was primarily for the opportunity to observe, and to put these lessons side by side with her other experiences throughout the past year.

There were a few items that she noticed she started to like about the office structure as she gained more outside expertise. One of these items was a three-layer review process that minimized the amount of errors. She decided that she wanted to exploit this concept in the future, but she would twist it by structuring the layers not based on ranking (junior staff, senior staff, managers), but on personality and skills. Detail-oriented folks needed to stay on top of the data entry, employees with high analytical skills needed to review the financials, and visionaries had to make sure the results that were derived and tied in with the client's vision. Whether this idea was viable or not, she didn't know, but it was worth trying, like any other.

***

January marked the beginning of the most difficult period in the Girl's life, both physically and mentally. Between the BooXkeeping clients, the tremendous growth of Universal Distributions, and tax work in Walter Diggin's office, she had her hands full. For the next four months she was chained to her chair once again, doing dreadful debit/credit work for 16 hours per day, seven days a week. In fact, this was beyond difficult. It was a nightmare. Monday through Thursday she needed to analyze, brainstorm, and complete mundane day-to-day bookkeeping work. On Friday and Saturday she was constantly under pressure to complete her tax-related office tasks with double the speed, so she could have time to answer business-related e-mails and requests during regular hours in such a way that her clients would feel no gaps in communication. Sundays were torn between the kids and more work, more QuickBooks, more financial statements.

There was no time for proper sleep. There was no time for social life or self-reflection. There was no time for Max. At first, Max tried really hard to understand and relate to her frustrations. After all, BooXkeeping was their mutual business, and he knew it would require a lot of dedication to build. He would make sure that one night a week, on Friday, the Girl shut down the computer and went out on sporadic dates with him. But she was too exhausted to enjoy these outings. She was running on 4-5 hours of sleep every night on weekdays and weekends, and that was wearing her out. She would get up and sit in front of the computer from 7am to 2am, with short breaks for food, restroom, and goodnight kisses for the kids. The joy in her demeanor was deteriorating. So was her love for life, and the healthy understanding of the reasoning behind why they decided to run this business.

She had no time to be with her kids or to run free. One night in early March before bedtime, her six-year old son came to her and asked:

"Mom, are we slaves?" It was an innocent question to him, with a purely philosophical meaning to her. Only kids are capable of asking these questions in such an open way.

"Why are you asking, sweetie?" She said carefully, kissing him on the forehead.

"Well, the other day we were learning in school about Abraham Lincoln and slavery. So our teacher was telling us how the slaves worked so hard for vast amounts of hours, slept very little, and didn't have the time or freedom to do anything they wanted or enjoyed. I am looking at you continually working at your computer all day long, I don't get to see you or spend time with you at all. So, it reminded me of the teacher's explanation."

She made a colossal effort not to cry at his answer and to give him instead some kind of reassuring and loving clarification for what was going on in their family these days. But that night she couldn't sleep, despite her fatigue. Yes, it was their business, but at this point it was a money machine that not only wasn't working properly just yet, but also required an amazing amount of hours and patience to operate. Was her son subconsciously right? Was she really becoming a slave to her own business? Waking up every morning was a challenge in itself, but if a year ago she didn't want to wake up because she had nothing to look forward to, this year it was hard due to physical and mental exhaustion.

She was progressing professionally. Jake's company just went through an extensive annual audit, and it was a great real-life test of whether the system she created for Universal Distributions was as good as she designed it to be. She aced this test. The audit was completed within one week, with one adjusting journal entry for depreciation, which is as close as it gets to a miracle in the accounting world. In the Walter Diggins office, she finally mastered the world of cash flows that had been a mystery to her since college, and she was quick to turn this knowledge around and construct five-year projection plans with built-in financial statements for a few of her BooXkeeping clients. Moreover, she was able to hire and train a part-time data entry person to help her with growing volume, and thus bring some order in the chaos of the business operations. But the more she progressed, the less desire she had to continue it all. She quit doing the events due to lack of time. With that, she sadly buried the creative, dreaming part of herself somewhere between the papers and numbers. She felt an emotional split inside, like her excited and blissful self was exiled to one world, while the analytical and practical self was overdeveloping in the other, in such a way that it almost resembled a tumor. And the two worlds inside her were completely disconnected, leaving her unhappy, empty, and distant.

Max felt the distance. He's had enough of it. He comprehended every reason behind what was happening between them. But on a gut level, he wanted attention. He wanted love. He was craving his wife. He needed the family as a whole again. As the season progressed, the more tired she felt, the more demanding Max would become of her attention, the more controlling and less supportive he would appear. Instead of conversations they had fights; instead of dates they had heavy silent periods. Everything seemed to go right logically, from a business standpoint, but ended up feeling wrong internally.

"Alex, I think I am losing it..." The Girl alleged, sitting in Alex's office, drinking tea by the fireplace and looking out the window at the hazy grey skies.

She had been out of touch with him, as well as the rest of the world, for a long time due to her workload, and it felt peaceful to see him again. It always felt peaceful to see him. With Alex in the room, her world would somehow mysteriously turn from chaotic motion into a subject with form and shape that oddly made sense. It was the very beginning of April; she was two weeks away from the end of the season, and she was praying to the Universe and God together for a change. She had just told him about the strange emotional split inside her, and so she continued the flow of thoughts.

"I mean, it's physical at this point. You know how much I love dancing, but last week I went out to a Zumba class, and my body literally felt split, like my upper body wasn't connected to my lower body. It's weird. And this type of work that I do... I mean, occasionally I learn something new, but mostly... I can do these transactions in my sleep without waking up. My mind stopped growing. I don't have any time to read or do anything else to feed it mentally. And the kids... I feel guilty every time I see them because I know I can't be with them for longer than 10 minutes. I gotta work some more. I hate feeling guilty... I don't remember the last time Max and I went to bed together because I always work so late or so early. I miss him... I have to slow myself down constantly. Otherwise I can't relate at the level I'm at right now. It's like I'm standing in the runway ready to take off for a flight, but as soon as I start gaining speed, someone tells me I need to stop, turn off the engine and practice some more. My problem is I kept playing along for the past year and a half because I had no choice. Alex, I just can't do it any longer. I *can't be slow anymore. It's not me, it's not my pace. This never-ending repetitive slow motion is draining me, it's eating me inside, the true passionate me, I mean...*"

Her thoughts were scattered, but it felt good to confess. Normally, the Girl and Max had a very honest, deep, and open relationship, and they could always share with each other what they really felt. But now that was unattainable. Max acted out about the tiniest things she would forget; he wasn't able to listen or to stay objective without taking what she said personally. And she had no energy whatsoever to pet anybody's ego. She could not rely on his mental support at this point. She was on the edge, but with that, she needed to appear strong, decisive, composed, and at least partially cheerful at home, so that Max and the boys wouldn't see how impossibly hard all of this really was for her, and how much she had to keep inside in order to keep going daily.

"What do I do?" She asked, glancing at Alex. Frequently, he had no problem interrupting to take a lead in the conversation, but for the last half hour of her sporadic monologue he had been unusually still behind his desk, playing with the pen in his fingers.

"Give it a month or two. It will all sort itself out."

"Promise?" The little girl inside her ached for someone to hold her hand, comb her hair, and tell her that everything would be OK, as illusory as it may have sounded for a 28-year-old woman.

Welcome to the Circle of Blindness.

6

DEFINING THE LINES

By April 15 Max and the Girl were drifting further and further apart. They tried to patch things up the old way. They bought two tickets to Chicago and decided to reconnect during a four-day trip. But that didn't work. Though Chicago in April was candidly charming with its multicolored beds of tulips, strong spring winds, and mysterious jazz bars, the Girl was so exhausted mentally and physically that four days away weren't nearly enough for her to recover her energy, let alone reconnect with Max. She needed a strong and dramatic shift to shake her world, dot all the i's and cross the t's.

The solution came from Jake. Universal Distributions was growing terrifically. He was in the process of expanding the operations to New York, hiring more staff, negotiating additional financing for the company. They were also exploring the option of upgrading the inventory system and moving it out of QuickBooks into industry specific software. Jake needed the Girl to fly in to the New York office for audits, hiring interviews, and implementation trainings. The challenging part was that she needed to be in the city three times, three to four days each, within a five week period. She had no idea how to balance this with her own clients; nor did she know exactly how to arrange it with Max and the kids. But saying "no" was not an option either, because by then she had put so much love and effort into the growth of Universal Distributions that she wasn't going to object. She wanted this company to succeed; *she had to see it succeed.*

And as destiny would have it, what seemed like a small diversion (in the form of a series of business trips) ended up spurring one of the thorniest, most unexpected, and most challenging growth spurts in her personal and professional life.

The Girl was crazy about the theater. Max had introduced her to musicals when they were just dating about 10 years ago, and since then they have been inseparable from the theater. Though she liked more philosophical, unconventional and deep productions (most often plays), Max taught her to appreciate the classical beauty of light-hearted musicals. New York, to her, was the epicenter of theater culture, especially musical theater. If she could name each trip separately, she would do so after the songs in Broadway productions that she either saw in New York during those trips, or that she came across through a gesture of fate while there.

"I'll be Surprisingly Good For You"

By the time her first trip rolled around in the middle of May, the Girl was in desperate need of a new experience. Due to the amount of actual technical work she completed, she was stuck in the day-to-day routine of the business. Max was working on the development of the business concept. That was the original agreement. However, they shortly learned that their roles within BooXkeeping were not fulfilled correctly. The Girl possessed an interesting combination of skills: she was technically knowledgeable and needed to stay on top of the operations, but on the flip side, she was an inspirational and conceptual leader, who carried conversations with her peculiarities, her free spirit, originality, and passion for life. Max was a great salesman: true, caring, and kind. But he was no visionary who could bring freshness into the business. He was a manager gifted by God, who was brilliant in monitoring any day-to-day activities. But since only part of each one of them was plugged in correctly, the other part was loose and unattached. This mismatch in responsibilities led to major dissatisfaction on both ends, and big conflict between the two. Moreover, it was extremely hard to separate the business and the personal sides of their existence. In fact, it was almost impossible, because when they worked and slept together, when they talked about love and business concurrently, when their office was their home and vice versa, how could they know when to stop and switch gears? *How do you train yourself to separate a lover, a husband or wife, and a business partner, who all have the same face and body, and while you are upset at one, stay happy with the other?*

When it was time to go to New York for the first time, the Girl couldn't wait to get away by herself. She promised herself to breathe in the city like there was no tomorrow. She needed to recharge, and she always recharged by herself. But there was another small factor that made this trip especially electrifying for her. When she was a teenager, she always thought that only "cool" people could go on business trips, especially to big cities like New York. She would read hundreds of novels about travelling executives; then she would lie in her bed late at night and dream of how she would participate in business meetings when she grew up, wearing high heels and sleek outfits, taking out her notepad to make key notes (iPads weren't around back then), and having weighty conversations. Adolescent fantasy, you know. And then, all of a sudden, in her own eyes, she transitioned from a distant bookkeeper with a conviction to make a business work into this "cool" person she knew; this "cool" person she was becoming. After this trip, she could go back to that teenager inside of her and honestly say: "You know what, you did it. You are cool!" *It might not sound like much to talk to a teenager inside of you and confirm to her that she is cool, but it is one of the most tearful, self-reflecting experiences.*

There was more to her bittersweet enthusiasm. Due to Max's decline in moral support and increase in demands, self-esteem justifications and constant bickering about her faults, the Girl needed to feel free and adventurous — to wake-up her inner self after 4-5 months of business "imprisonment." She also sharply ached for being needed and accepted just the way she was, which she wasn't getting at home for the time being, despite how much she and Max loved each other deep inside. That made her open and vulnerable to anyone who would simply let her be. New York and Universal Distributions were a perfect setup.

Jake always let her be. Whether he was open-minded and accepting in such a superb capacity, or he just never cared enough, she could never tell. But it didn't matter, because for that trip it was exactly what she needed. She needed someone to leave her alone and let her do her thing. As a result, she completely immersed herself in New York, at that time of year, and at that time of her life. She gave more than she possessed for the audit and the hiring interviews, and everything excited her: the people, the rain, the food, the unregulated hours—for no real cause other than Universal Distributions' prosperity. She had a desperate hunger for excitement and joy to fill the void, to take home as a source of energy. One night she was talking to a waitress in an Argentinean restaurant, and the conversation carried away into an argument about the life beliefs, big ideas and human choices in an exuberating, truth-seeking and theoretical manner that was standard for the Girl. The waitress asked her, with a gasp.

"What do you do for living? Are you a writer?"

"No," the Girl smiled. "I'm an accountant."

She was catching herself a lot lately feeling painfully aware of how awkward she really was: too philosophical for an accountant, too investigative for an artist: *misfit in both worlds*.

That time in New York, among other musicals, she saw *Evita*. Her favorite song had always been "I'll Be Surprisingly Good for You", but at that moment the song reminded her of herself, wanting to be surprisingly good, to belong in something real, profitable, and grand like what Universal Distributions was growing into, to have a part of her embedded into a story with a "happy ending."

...It seems crazy but you must believe
There's nothing calculated, nothing planned
Please forgive me if I seem naive
I would never want to force your hand
But please understand, I'd be good for you.

I don't always rush in like this
Twenty seconds after saying hello
Telling strangers I'm too good to miss
If I'm wrong I hope you'll tell me so
But you really should know, I'd be good for you
I'd be surprisingly good for you...

(From "I'll Be Surprisingly Good For You", *Evita*, 1973)

"The Hill"

The energy she derived from the first trip didn't last. In fact, as soon as the Girl came home and hit reality, she couldn't wait to run away to New York again in a week. She felt like she was betraying her home, her husband, her kids, her business. What was really happening was that she was craving any kind of thrill and mental stimulation, and unlike home life, with its daily challenges, stupid fights, strenuous routines, unspoken feelings, and restless nights, New York trips supplied her with plenty of everything she lacked at home. It almost felt like an overdose of mental and emotional stimulant, and she occasionally wondered whether it could be used as a lethal weapon.

Max felt the difference in her energy, but could not pinpoint it. They'd been together long enough where they were able to just sense each other. So in subconscious return, for the week that she was home, he become even more upset, irritated, controlling; he demanded even more attention every moment, blamed her for spending too much time on Universal Distributions and other work, claiming that her passion for challenge was being used by Jake for the benefit of his company and she was too naive and stubborn to see it. The connection between the two was becoming thinner and thinner. It was getting harder and harder for the Girl to keep on loving this man despite his accusations: loving the man she knew, not the man she saw.

Her second trip to New York had a completely different meaning to her. She went to New York to escape herself, to avoid the upsetting environment of home and the absence of creativity in the business. She hoped that New York would give her some energy this time around as well. Instead, she felt completely lonely and on edge.

As karma would have it, as soon as she left for New York, all of BooXkeeping's clients suddenly needed everything done right then and there, which was impossible because she was investing ungodly hours in Universal Distributions, and there was no one else to finish the tasks on both sides.

The hiring interviews were useful and remarkable from a professional growth standpoint. The Girl met various people and was allowed the autonomy to ask any questions she wanted, to lead the meetings in any way she desired. She was toying with Jake's approach of hiring by energy, and she was fascinated by the experience. But the position for which Universal

Distributions was hiring was that of a full-time controller, which made her feel replaced and unneeded. After all that she had built within Universal Distributions, it was like whiplash to her heart.

She went through the software implementation training. She had done implementations before, and they had always been exceptionally entertaining for her. She liked playing with puzzles, putting the pieces together when they seemed to be in a complete commotion, building a fortress from a mountain of rubble. But, whereas during her first trip she was feverish about the vision of the business success of Universal Distributions and herself as part of it, now she sharply realized that the "happy ending" would happen without her. And this realization was just throbbing. It felt like growing somebody else's baby: when you give all your love to it knowing in the back of your mind that it doesn't belong to you, and at some point in the near future the parents are going to come and claim this baby, leaving your heart hurting and bleeding.

To top it off, at the end of her trip, before the decision on the candidates was made, Jake had made her a job offer for the same Controller position for which they were hiring.

"You are my number one choice, the Girl," he said to her at a bar. "As long as you do the job, you wouldn't hear a peep out of me."

This was much worse than feeling replaced. *It was a right of first refusal*, something that she respected a lot more than money or status. And the truth was that this offer a year or five years ago would have been a dream to the Girl: the money, the flexibility, the trips, and the challenge–everything was there. She should have felt a great pride, but she felt completely empty and sad inside. She knew deep in her heart that if she took the offer, Max would be thrilled, because it would finally bring long-term stability into their lives. But with that, she would be betraying herself and her fuzzy vision of true freedom, which didn't include a full-time job. She had to face the hardest decision in her professional life, as well as the consequences of this choice later on. She declined the offer. She just couldn't go against herself anymore. And declining felt like ripping herself apart: *her mind was upset at her heart for not being able to make another family sacrifice.*

Max was speechless when he found out that she declined the offer. "Hope you know what you are doing, because at this point I don't understand it," he said. With that, the last thread in their connection was torn for good.

So there the Girl was: running a business that took up all of her personal and family time, being blown away by a project that neither belonged to her, nor satisfied her role financially, and left her completely disconnected from the man who was supposed to be by her side no matter what, but wasn't. Her heart knew that not taking the offer would ultimately bring her more tranquility over time, but at that moment she felt that it marked the beginning of a free fall. Just like in skydiving, there was no going back after the jump. She was all alone on this journey to figure it all out professionally and personally, on her own, without a hint of light at the end of the tunnel. She left New York weeping.

During that trip, the Girl went out to see the musical *Once*, a touching love story between two people who worked on a music project together and were drawn to one another, yet had no courage to take action, and needed to let go in the end to be able to complete their journeys. She felt the same way, only not to a certain person, but to a company: to Universal Distributions, the project that gave her all the thrills that she desired, and more. Yet, to move forward, she needed to let go of that high feeling, and search for her own happiness in the world back at home. *She was climbing the hill, all scratched and burned, excited to witness the hill itself, instead of feeling exhilaration for the vision behind it.*

Walking up the hill tonight
when you have closed your eyes.
I wish I didn't have to make
all those mistakes and be wise.
Please try to be patient
and know that I'm still learning.
I'm sorry that you have to see
the strength inside me burning.

But where are you my angel now?
Don't you see me crying?
And I know that you can't do it all
but you can't say I'm not trying...

(From "The Hill", *Once*, 2012)

"I Am What I Am"

The Girl came home depressed. Max could feel it. But he couldn't understand why. And as any man in love would do, Max started looking for an explanation where he should not have. He became jealous, thinking that there was more to the New York trips than just Universal Distributions and excitement from it. And she was just fed up. She had no desire to express or defend herself. He interfered with her business tactics and questioned her every professional and personal move. She turned inward. He treated her with very little significance at home, blaming her for not spending time with him or the kids, choosing other people or other pleasures instead. She ignored him and worked some more. He gave her no credit for what she did, picking on her every action and being upset instead. She pretended not to care. He wanted her to give up the New York project and quit right then and there, even though it brought in a substantial amount of money for their budget. She couldn't handle it any more. She was going to finish the project with no further discussion. She never took orders from anyone; no one owned her. She hit the bottom.

True love is a combination of pretty happiness, ugly happiness, pretty sadness and ugly sadness; often it's hard to tell them apart, but to advance as a couple, you need to go through all the stages.

When someone tells you that if you meet "the one," you will live happily ever after, forever loving, wanting, and respecting this one person, don't believe them. They haven't known long-term love. Love comes in cycles. When you keep evolving on an individual level, you occasionally question and test the validity of "the one," of your impacts on each other's lives, of the quality of your relationship and the true origins of your connection. You are not a hero at these moments; in fact, you are most likely perceived as a selfish bitch or a brutal asshole. And that's OK, because this is the only way to keep maturing together as a couple. And if you don't, you end up in a filthy pond called habitual existence. Some people live in that pond their whole lives, because they are afraid to face the truth and deal with it.

The Girl was a few inches away from walking out on everything that mattered in her life: Max, the business, trips, and Universal Distributions. But to walk away meant to be defeated. *She refused to allow any of these circumstances to break her.* She had to go back to New York in two weeks to train a new controller. And, sure as hell, she was going to do it.

After a few sleepless nights with the sour taste of whiskey in her mouth, she realized what had happened, when it happened, and why it happened. Then, instead of losing herself, she decided to pull herself together.

Every subject is designed with sharply defined lines. Take a table, for example. It might be covered with a heavy tablecloth and might blend in with the rest of the interior, looking like a whole, but as soon as you put a book on the edge of it, the book is going to fall because it crossed the line, or rather it crossed the space where the table was OK with supporting its weight. Pure physics in a creative form. Can you use the table for other purposes? Of course. It can become a shelf, a cutting board, or even a hideaway spot if you are willing to climb underneath. But nothing changes the lines that define the table. Can you redesign the table? Yes. But a redesigned version of the same table has other well-defined lines, that represent the continuation of the original lines. What happened to the Girl was primitively genius. When she went out to her first interview, pushed by the necessity to support the family, she accepted the fact that her lines needed modification in order to fit into the world out there. But instead of redefining the lines, she allowed other people to blur them to the point of invisibility, like a washed-out pencil drawing. *If there is no line, there is nothing to cross; thus anything becomes permissible.*

It was time to redefine, and in a few cases reshape, or even expand the lines of her character. But this time they would be printed in ink.

The Girl started off with the longest and the toughest conversation she had ever had with Max. They needed to accept the fact that they had to work out this matter on both personal and business levels because to be happy together, it was crucial to fix both worlds.

In the business, they agreed that they both needed their kingdoms of expertise, where their roles where separated, and while one person was a primary decision maker, the other would be secondary. In this case, they would develop a feeling of ownership in what they did in their own realm, therefore being OK to submit and support the other kingdom. They needed to learn to leave and respect each other's space. How come these basic lessons are not taught in business school for Management 101?

They discussed personal issues. It was detrimental and heart-breaking to realize that their connection actually started tearing right after that conversation in Starbucks. Max couldn't forgive himself subconsciously for making the Girl chase work in the accounting field alongside the people with an inflexible mind-frame. He was a merciful protector by nature; yet ironically, this time he couldn't protect the woman he loved more than anything from the failure of helplessly trying to fit into a world where she was neither welcomed nor understood. In a way, he wanted her to be mad at him for doing this; he would almost prefer her to be mad. But the Girl was not mad at all. She had taken it for granted that it had been her time to step up and pull the family out of the hole they were in. She just wanted to be held, and kissed, and loved, and accepted at least in the warmth of her own home and his arms, just as windy as she was. That would give her enough strength to go on with not fitting, not being understood, and ultimately not caring for any of it as long as the results were there.

They also talked about how little they really loved each other in the last year. If you never read *The Five Love Languages* by Gary Chapman, you have missed out on one of wisest books of humanity. The book talks about the different ways people perceive love: through words, presents, actions, time spent together, and touch. Max felt loved by spending time together, and the Girl felt loved by being touched. So where she could get away with a hug, Max needed a full blown date. Together they decided to introduce a 10-second rule into their daily routine: they had to hold each other really tight for at least 10 seconds, thus for at least 10 seconds every day she was being touched while he was spending time with her.

There was no major shift after the conversation. *The more two people love each other, the longer it takes to heal the wounds.* But now at least there was a glimpse of hope.

On the plane to New York, the Girl was thinking about Universal Distributions. She had been trying to get a hold of Jake for two weeks with no success. She was now working full days just on his company, between the implementation, audits, reporting, and other tasks, which was far beyond their initial agreement. She didn't mind the load; she was sincerely jazzed about the growth of this company, and carried away with challenges. Her mind was finally working full force at the appropriate speed: learning, comprehending, analyzing. But the incentives that kept her going were purely due to her own nature. Jake didn't add to those incentives at all. On the contrary, lack of communication with Jake was slowly shedding away the pleasure she received from Universal Distributions. After all, it was the growth of *his* company that she was working on, and at least feedback would be appreciated.

When she came to New York and tried to reach out to him again, he briefly replied that he didn't have time. She recognized the familiar sign: her lines got blurred here as well. Somehow she made it acceptable for him to act this way. She felt like she was wasting her time and efforts. *When a tiger is backed in a corner, he fights fiercely because he has nothing more to lose.* Neither did the Girl.

When Jake called her regarding a business issue the same day, she was outrageously pissed at him for his non-responsiveness. But then, listening to him rambling about payables and receivables, she contemplated deep inside her that if the Universe was fair, and if she threw the message into its proximities, assuming that she was doing everything the way it was meant to be, the Universe would reply to her. So holding back her anger, she told Jake frankly that she was upset with him.

"What do you mean you are upset with me? Girl, you never get upset with me!" He tried to joke his way out.

"Well, then there is first time for everything." She answered firmly. It was time to redefine the lines.

They agreed to have dinner together after work. They started off on a rough note. She sucked at hiding her rage, and he was just picking up and reflecting her mood with his own behavior. So they had one argument after another before they finally reached the gist of the issue. The Girl explained to him that she was excited about the progress of what they had accomplished in the past year within Universal Distributions, but his lack of feedback and connection made her feel like what she did, and ultimately she herself, didn't matter. She yearned to understand whether he just didn't care or whether he was so preoccupied with his own world that he never had a chance to see her side of things. She needed an answer at once. She was ready for either answer, as long as there was an answer.

"I am passionate about Universal Distributions, Jake. I love what I create here, I am passionate to the point that it burns my heart with the desire to move forward. But when you are silent and ignorant, I feel like I am hitting a wall, time after time, after time. It makes me want to shut the door and never come back." She quietly said, with tears in her eyes.

The Girl was entirely open during this conversation, to the point of internal nakedness, when you just know that you are hitting pure truth by staying absolutely honest to yourself, which at that instant means a world more than the outcome itself.

And, the Universe magically gave the answer to her. Jake's features softened right away, and he opened up. He explained to her where he was coming from and what was on his mind. They spoke for another two hours about his personal matters, the growth, vision, and future of Universal Distributions, and some other unrelated subjects. Their conversations often drifted into philosophical and idealistic horizons, and this time was no exception. At the end of the night, when Jake was leaving, he turned to her at the door, and said "Good night, sweetie." Then he stopped and gazed at her for a moment before he strolled out. It wasn't what he said, but how he said it: the way a loving older brother would talk to his young sister: with the utmost care and responsibility, with gentle strength and human love. And she… she was just grateful for this moment, grateful to him and to the Universe, because two hours prior she had been desperate for the supernatural feeling that the divine was on her side, so she could regain energy and move forward in every aspect of her life, however rigid it might be again.

The next morning, she woke up her happy and joyful self, ready to conquer the world. As she was walking to the New York office, she couldn't get the song out of her head from yet another musical *La Cage aux Folles*. The name of the song was "I Am What I Am."

I am what I am
I am my own special creation.
So come take a look,
Give me the hook or the ovation.
It's my world that I want to take a little pride in,
My world, and it's not a place I have to hide in.
Life's not worth a damn,
'Til you can say, "Hey world, I am what I am."

I am what I am,
I don't want praise, I don't want pity.
I bang my own drum,
Some think it's noise, I think it's pretty.
And so what, if I love each feather and each spangle,
Why not try to see things from a diff'rent angle?
Your life is a sham 'til you can shout out loud
I am what I am!

I am what I am
And what I am needs no excuses.
I deal my own deck

Sometimes the ace, sometimes the deuces.
There's one life, and there's no return and no deposit;
One life, so it's time to open up your closet.
Life's not worth a damn 'til you can say,
"Hey world, I am what I am!"

(From "I Am What I Am", *La Cage Aux Folles*, 2008)

7

TWO PLUS ONE

The Girl came home reenergized and oddly rejuvenated. Nothing had seriously changed in her life since four days before her third trip to New York. But her attitude had changed. She felt unstoppable. She was ready to go forward in spite of any obscure obstacles that might appear in her path.

Her relationship with Max was on a stretched recovery program. As soon as she came back, they left for a pre-planned 10-day trip to Munich and Prague to reconnect and do the things they loved the most: immerse themselves in unknown cities, languages, food, and customs; talk with each other, drink wine, meet up with friends, and sightsee. They loved to travel; it was another passion of theirs. But even more so, they loved to travel together, because like authentic partners-in-crime, there was nothing they didn't want to try or experience mutually, and that aspiration had always added fantastic memories to their relationship. So for the whole 10 days, the couple was catching up on what they had missed in the last year of each other's lives. It wasn't a swift comeback to where they were a year ago. Instead, it was a development into a new, more mature phase in their relationship: where two people accept the fact that they will occasionally hurt each other, but the desire to wake up every morning next to this person is prevailing over anything else.

The Girl still had to do some work while they were on vacation. Business was business. But unlike last year in Boston, she wasn't glued to the computer anymore. She could choose timing that suited her schedule to complete her tasks. Besides, her time was divided 50/50 between Universal Distributions and her own clients, and that was another positive diversion. She was no longer dependent on one company; she started diversifying, which was the healthiest thing in the money-making process. One of the most signature moments of the trip was the time when she had to finish some urgent projections for a client. They found a restaurant with free wi-fi (it was a prerequisite), but, as an added benefit, the restaurant served the best beef tartar they had tried in ages, spread over a fresh roasted garlic toast, dipped in marinated cheeses, with a bottle of excellent white wine and a couple espressos to go with that, offered on a patio overlooking a beautiful cathedral square. Yes, the Girl was still working, but working with this view and in these circumstances in the heart of Europe with the person you love next to you was a definite stretch, or rather big-time improvement, on the conditional freedom of the last year.

On her way back from the vacation the Girl caught herself thinking about happiness and what it meant to her. She had read a lot on how westerners associated happiness with money, status, and material goods, which was temporary; and easterners argued that happiness was a state of mind, which was trained and meditated on, so, as a result, it implied continuity and permanence. But to the Girl, none of these definitions were precise, because each one of them eliminated a very big beneficial part of what the other suggested. Western approach concentrated purely on the external factors, while Eastern approach raised internal significance above all. To her, though, the necessity of the presence of both concepts in her life was obvious. You can't concentrate on internal satisfaction if you have no food on the table for your children or no money to pay the bills, because your mind is searching for immediate solutions—in civilized survival mode. Yet, if you are only driven by power, money, and things for their own sake, and are surrounded by the people who respect you mostly for what you can afford to offer them at the moment (luxury, entertainment, etc), you lose the depth of meaning in your existence. She knew few people who were brave and intelligent enough to embrace both approaches in their worlds. Most often they ended up oscillating helplessly from one extreme to the other, like a ship in a bad storm. To the Girl, the balance, the essence of true happiness, laid in an organic combination of both theories.

Happiness is a choice. It is neither provided, nor meditated on. Happiness is a decision, an active state of mind, a daily ongoing wakeup call that makes you measure your own progress on your diverse happiness chart in any imaginable area of your life at any given moment, thus pushing yourself to grow both internally and externally.

Happiness is a three-step process:

Step 1. You accept the fact that any individual, starting with you, has a right to be happy. It's an axiom, a faith, a human birthright.

Step 2. You look at your life from all possible angles and honestly assess with an open mind in which areas you are not happy. Analytical and observational skills are the most useful here.

Step 3. You take actions in order to change the factors that make you unhappy, or you change your attitude toward those factors with a clear understanding of why you are doing it. All actions involve a risk of failure, a possibility of success, a responsibility to take care of the consequences — but most importantly, they give you contentment in ownership of the result, which ultimately is your own happiness.

Manifestation in itself is not going to relieve you from your unhappiness, and neither will the self-destructive theory of feeling obligated to suffer constantly just because other people around you suffer, live an unsatisfied life, and don't whine about it. This argument is doomed in its foundation, because it rejects the fact that life is about choices. It's their choice to live their lives however they find it fit. And it's your choice to be happy.

***

Unlike matters with Max, the business took a little dip before it started going up again. While the couple was on vacation in Europe, one of their significant clients called and asked for a copy of a file, which they could only get to him three-to-four days later due to a lack of connectivity, time difference, and unchangeable travel arrangements. The client was completely upset and requested to cancel his contract within two weeks.

It wasn't the first client that the Girl and Max had lost in the last year. There is always a natural process of a client turnover in any business model. However, this one was a painful loss. The reason was just as simple as it had been with their relationship or with Universal Distributions: the lines were never clearly defined. With this particular client, there were no clear boundaries on responsibilities and compensation. The couple had picked up this client back in winter, when they were taking any work without much thought towards the profitability of every single project. At that point the client needed a lot of work done, but going forward it should not have taken too much time. As the year went on, the client started growing very fast without a solid internal structure. So he was requesting more and more service, time, and effort on the BooXkeeping end of the spectrum. However, the terms were never renegotiated. A few of the immediate requests and conversations happened while she was flying back and forth from New York in early summer, and the client was outraged that the requested work wasn't completed right away, even though that was never part of the deal. So eventually he decided to find another bookkeeper.

The painful part was that though both parties were not exactly thrilled with the contract toward the end, one had decided to go, leaving the other party guessing. Had they had a conversation earlier on about these matters, clearly defining who was doing what, how it would be executed, on what timelines, and with what workforce, their business relationship might have emerged at a new level. But the client was located in a different state, often inaccessible for urgent requests, and wanted to focus on growth, instead of investing time in expressing himself a little more clearly to the team. And the Girl was too preoccupied with her own business to put a pause on the whole process, chase the client down, and state her point of view. What's gone is gone.

The Girl's initial reaction was emotional. She knew that she had contributed 120% of her effort on this client's project, and she had the urge to know why this had happened. Unfortunately, the mastery of a breakup, professional or personal, is only solved with experience. So it took the Girl a few days to go back in her memory and her mind, objectively evaluate this business relationship, and grasp the fact that there was nothing else she could do differently at this point, other than just learn from this mistake. This was the third case (after Max and Universal Distributions) in the course of a two-month period where she needed to clearly define the lines. It was definitely a sign that she needed to comprehend this lesson in her gut, as well as learn to do something about it instantaneously. So to avoid another reminder from the Universe, she decided to be proactive on the subject. She went back and reassessed all current contracts with the other clients. For some of them, she would need to go back and renegotiate openly, facing a chance of not being able to keep the client. In most cases, the clients that needed revisions were earlier clients, obtained when the Girl and Max were just establishing their margins in the business services that their company would be providing. The hardest client to face was going to be Freddie. By then she had worked for him for over a year, and there was a certain pattern already established in their business relationship and expectations.

She had completely passed the trust test by then and he treated her in many ways like a member of his family, as he would often concur himself. With that, he lacked an assistant; therefore he occasionally pushed office tasks onto her, like filing paperwork, or insurance rates negotiation, which she never agreed to perform. So the conversation wasn't easy. But when you are genuine in your arguments, the other party may not be happy about the changes, but will be more willing to accept your terms and work with you, thus resulting in a win-win negotiation scenario.

This learning curve of the objective review of her roles, her clients, and the validity of their contracts had also taught the Girl another very important concept.

We, as humans, perceive and learn from any experience in a *QQC progression: through the process of evolving from quantity, to quality, to connection.* We stay at the quantitative stage, or "the more, the merrier" stage, until we complete about 50-60 percent of the learning curve: we understand what the experience is about, we have gone through enough variety to distinguish what we like and don't like, or what works and what doesn't, and we have gained confidence in this experience. When we feel that we are ready to expand our experience further, we leap from the quantitative stage to the qualitative stage, where the number of occurrences is not as important as their consistent eminence. This stage takes us to the 60-85th percentile of the learning curve. By the end of this stage we are solid in our knowledge; we are comfortable with the experience, and satisfied with the repetitive, good, and sometimes even great results. The next stage, the evolution from the qualitative stage to the connected stage, is a much deeper, more intense, but continuous part of learning. It picks up learning from the 85th percentile and pushes it forward, or in other words, it transitions the experience from good and great to extraordinary. This part of the learning curve is the hardest, the most involved, the most unpredictable, but also the most rewarding.

QQC progression, like a ReVision Triangle, is a universal concept, which is applicable in both business and personal areas. Let's take travel, for example. When you arrive at a new city as a tourist, you are desperate to take the camera out and start taking photos and videos. You photograph or film anything and everything that might be of the slightest interest: the sunset, a monument, strangers, buildings, art, streets, landscapes, signs, etc. You make hundreds of images, before you realize that by taking so many photos you actually are not letting yourself enjoy the city in its natural beauty. So as the next step, you become selective in what you capture. You now pay more attention to what you see and hear versus how it's going to look in a photo. Hence, you allow yourself to dig deeper into the experience of the city.

The final stage happens when you accept the fact that all the photos and videos are great, but they are only visual (occasionally audio) representations of your travel experience. By busying yourself with the camera, you don't let yourself plunge into the depths of the experience. So at that point, you put the camera away, and that's when the real experience starts: when you smell the flowers in the city, listen to the unfamiliar sounds of the streets, unwrap your taste buds to new and unexplored foods, sit on a bench for few hours gazing at the trees and architecture, people-watching, admiring the uniqueness of this city and the way it embraces you. This is how true memories are created, imprinted on a multi-dimensional, gut level, which can neither be recorded nor retold.

Another more common example of the QQC Progression is the relationship experience. You start with a dating stage, or a quantitative stage. You date as many people as you can handle for your own taste, learning from the variety of mixed experiences. The next stage is when you grasp that long-term satisfaction lies in a quality relationship, so you look for a long-term commitment; you may even call it love. If before, you wanted more experiences and diversity of results, now you choose fewer experiences with more meaning and more predictable outcomes. In other words, as you progress, you start looking for depth and value in a relationship. True learning, the pinnacle of experience, comes when you find one person with whom you connect on such a deep, energetic level, that you neither look for variety, nor for predictability of the outcome. It's a completely different stage in the relationship, a stage which is beyond explanation, beyond description, beyond comprehension, where you are so bonded with the other person that you can't even elucidate it. This bond is called true love.

In business, just like it was in the Girl's case, the QQC progression is applicable to the client-finding process. When you open the business, you take any possible or impossible clients to work out the model and start the process. Some of them might not be profitable, others are too demanding. Eventually, as you grow professionally, you naturally select the clients that fit your perfect market and are satisfied with your services. You understand that you would rather have reliable and happy repeating customers, than a never-ending assortment of new customers. And for the most part, these quality customers conclude your client list. The exception to this list is a handful of clients, with whom, for whatever reasons, you have built a strong internal connection to the point where, though they might not be your best or most profitable clients, you choose to keep them because the relationship is beyond pure professionalism. You are growing with them in some unexpected ways, just as they grow with you. And this bond is very valuable and special to you, even if it may lead to completely unexpected outcomes. In her business, the Girl had passed the quantitative stage between winter and spring, and by defining the lines, she leaped into the qualitative stage of client list creation. With Jake and Freddie, she had already established a connection. And she was getting ready to convert some more quality client relationships into long-lasting meaningful connections.

As a side note, not everybody completes all three stages of the QQC progression. The majority end up somewhere between the quantitative and qualitative stages of the learning curve. They opt out for the known, shallow varieties of the first part, or the solid predictability of the second part, both of which usually fall within their comfort zone. Very few individuals are ready to keep going forward in the direction of the unknown: the vicinity of real connections.

***

Things finally started to look up. Universal Distributions made good, steady progress. The new software implementation had slowly started, as did the new controller. He was carefully picking up on the company requirements and expectations, as well as day-to-day tasks and deadlines.

The BooXkeeping client list was growing linearly. The Girl continued to commit her 120% of effort to every client that she worked with. The events of the early summer had taught her the importance of staying true to herself; *in the cyclical chaos of what she had to deal with on a professional basis, the internal axis of her flexible but unbreakable core was occasionally the only constant of the process.* And as a result the feedback from the clients finally started to come in as an answer to her actions. "You have too much personality for a bookkeeper," one client said after a half-hour long conversation on the subject of human happiness. "You are like that thing that you dread buying for a very long time, but then you can't imagine how you lived without it," another client commented: the same client who was hesitant to switch from the owner-based bookkeeping process via Excel to a QuickBooks oriented system that saved precious time for the owner, but also provided extended reporting capacity.

The workload had picked up along with the client list. At this point, the Girl wasn't able to do all the work in BooXkeeping herself. While she did have a part-time person working on the basic clients, this no longer covered the ongoing regular needs of the weekly and bi-weekly customers. It was time to not only grow BooXkeeping, but also grow within BooXkeeping. So Max and the Girl finally decided they were ready to hire their first full-time employee.

The Girl had a dream mock-up of the employee in her mind, which was a combination of two very different people she has met through her work engagements. One of them was a super-efficient assistant in Universal Distributions that kept an enormous amount of details in her head, and was very thorough and fast. The other person was a parking attendant in Freddie's building. The woman had worked for the company that owned the parking structure for a very long time, and had no problem chasing a car for a five dollar payment around the parking lot, or giving a short but pertinent lecture on a 2-day late check for the monthly parking space. She was so incredibly loyal and diligent that she earned the greatest respect for what she did. The Girl needed someone with the efficiency of the assistant and the work ethic of the parking attendant, but also with composed and positive energy.

They posted the advertisement on Craigslist (God bless Craig Newmark!). After a series of interviews, Max and the Girl had found a perfect fit: a young woman with an accounting degree, who planned to become CPA in the future but was interested in starting with the basics and working her way up in accounting knowledge. She was very detail oriented, skilled in Excel, liked the variety that different industries would provide, was willing to learn, and was genuinely positive.

BooXkeeping was really shaping into a profitable start-up. Thanks to the new employee, in addition to another bookkeeper that contracted for them, the Girl was finally able to more or less control her priorities in her business and personal life, and manage the workload. And while Universal Distributions was still taking up way more time than was originally agreed upon, her workdays in general became somewhat shorter and more ordered — a structure that was designed in a way that fit her and suited her beliefs and her lifestyle. For the first time in the last year and a half, the colors of the Girl's life finally gained some brightness and liveliness. On a personal level, the couple now made a point of spending more time together; they resumed their one or two day stayacation getaways to stay connected. It always felt great to come back home with more fun memories.

It was on one of those trips to LA, when they were having a discussion about something relevant and irrelevant to business, that the Girl fell suddenly silent in mid-sentence, and looked at Max mesmerized, like she just hit a goldmine without ever getting out of the car.

"Max, do you remember that guy from Jamaica?" She whispered in awe.

"What guy from Jamaica?" He asked her, trying to concentrate on the road.

"C'mon, *the guy*, from Jamaica... You know who I'm talking about!" She suddenly looked like a hyperactive buoyant teenager, glowing with excitement.

About four years ago, during their stay at a resort in Jamaica, the couple had met a man in his early 60s. He was there with his gorgeous blond European girlfriend, and he carried himself with a contagious, authoritative aura of accomplishment and satisfaction in life. At some point they ended up in the bar together, and as often happens on vacation in a secluded resort, they started conversing with each other. The man asked them what they did for living, and Max told him about the construction business they ran at that time.

"What do you do?" Max asked him in return.

"*I do whatever I want to do.*" The man replied.

It turned out that the man had made his fortune buying and selling land and real estate in Texas or Arizona in the '80s and early '90s. But this phrase, this concept of living — "I do whatever I want to do" — had been haunting the couple ever since.

"What about him?" Max rejoined.

"Well, you know how we always associated this "I do whatever I want to do" lifestyle with him, in such a way that it was supposed to originate from the passive investment income that usually came at a more respectable age, with maturity and experience.

So honestly, it felt a little distant and unattainable to us. But it just hit me! Guess what... We don't need to be sixty or make money in real estate. Because that wasn't the meaning behind this message. Look at us right now: with the way we build BooXkeeping, our service business, and lead our lives between: kids, theater, exciting projects, and travel. *At our financial and personal level today, we already do whatever we want to do!"*

8

PARANORMAN

This chapter of the Girl's life was very brief, but so vivid and out of this world, similar to an orgasm, that without it the whole story would be absolutely pastel and flat. This ecstatic feeling doesn't usually last for a long time; it is extremely short-lived in its nature, but it is absolutely essential for the wholeness of an experience. It represents the highest point of an experience, when everything just feels undeniably right, like it's supported by unknown supernatural forces.

For the Girl, this vibrant section of her life consisted of two major parts: the headstand, and the last New York trip of this ReVision Triangle.

***

Back in May, during her first trip to New York, Jake and the Girl had breakfast right before she flew back home. As always, the conversation went astray into the general subjects, and at some point she asked him about his involvement with yoga practice, as well as his reasoning and take on the subject. She was always curious about the "why" of things, and she could feel the internal progression within him in the last year, so she attributed it to regular yoga practice. Jake was happy to share. Yoga was his true passion, one that only comes from long-term attachment and acquired taste. So he started to explain to the Girl the concepts behind yoga practice, the nature of the experience, and the emotions that it awoke or, on the contrary, subdued. The Girl remembered that part of their breakfast clearly, like it was yesterday, because it felt completely surreal.

They were seated outside in a small Belgian café, and it was drizzling. As soon as Jake started talking to her about yoga, the weather changed. It became the heaviest, pouring rain she had seen in years. They couldn't move, as the space under the patio roof was very limited. They decided to wait out the rain, and he kept talking in a completely captivating manner, with gestures, examples, and quotes. You can only hear this kind of a story when a person not only wholeheartedly loves the subject of the conversation, but is also happily and deeply intertwined in it. Between the rain and the thrill of his tale, the energy felt so thick that you could cut it with a knife. It was imaginary: but the Girl could almost see this energy. It felt like the Universe was trying to tell her something extremely important through this story, like it had set up the weather and this breakfast to prove a central point to her. Have you ever felt that way? When you witness a complete alignment of nature with extracurricular circumstances, brought together in perfect unison, just for you? It's an indescribable feeling. The Girl couldn't tell how long it lasted, but the next few things she remembered, not necessarily in a connected manner, were the rain subsiding, the waitress pushing the bill across the table, and Jake laughing out loud.

"What are you laughing at?" The Girl asked him,

trying to come back to the reality of where she was.

"You. I think the waitress just snapped you out of it! Sorry." He tried really hard to stop chuckling. "It was just way too funny."

"I'm glad you're entertained." She mumbled back with an embarrassed smile. But her mind hadn't fully returned from the moment before. The experience was just too empowering.

"But seriously," Jake finished the conversation. "As open-minded as you are, I think you would love it. You should totally try it."

On her way back in the plane, she couldn't get over the feeling that the Universe was talking to her through Jake, and that she just needed to try this yoga activity that he was into. She couldn't explain why.

When she came back, she signed up for a few classes. She was never much of an athlete, so she was a little hesitant at first when she saw her fellow students doing handstands and headstands with the elegance of birds. She told herself that she'd be lucky to get somewhere close to a headstand within a year, but there was no way she was giving up now. She had to explore what was so magnificently meaningful in yoga practice.

Fast forward through a few months of irregular yoga classes, two or three times per week (that's all she could fit between kids and work), and the Girl was head-over-heels in love with this practice. On one hand, it was the only physical activity that connected her mind and her body. Before, she used to go jogging, or climb stairs in order to think. Her mind would escape, while her body worked out. In yoga, she wasn't able to do that because as soon as her mind drifted away, she would lose the concentration and fall. She had to learn to make her mind still and focused to stay balanced. On the other hand, she was always very flexible in her upper body, and never knew what to do with that skill. In yoga she could advance that flexibility, while developing strength. Just like in real life, she could deepen her flexibility and open-mindedness, while working on the strength of her character. In fact, her biggest challenge both inside and outside of yoga practice was not strength. It was having confidence in, and trusting herself: the convenient and solid gut feeling that she could trust herself to handle a task: a pose, a challenge. She needed to connect on a mental and physical level, and yoga was really instrumental in achieving that.

The accomplishments of these greatly treasured practices culminated in her very first headstand only two months later. She had been working on it almost every day, by the wall at home, even when she didn't practice a full yoga series, and at one session she was finally able to go up with the teacher's help. First of all, she never thought she'd be able to do it so soon, and that was an achievement in itself. But there was more to it.

In a headstand, looking upside down at everything around her.... *For the first time in 28 years, her world finally snapped into place and looked normal!* It was as if she had been searching for a hiding place where she could feel normal, and she found it at last here, in the upside down state. She realized that she obviously couldn't live in this state forever; she actually couldn't even stay there for a very long time, but at least she knew where to go when she needed to straighten herself out. It was one of her biggest and the most significant personal discoveries. Would she ever have found this hiding place if it weren't for that breakfast in the rain? Who knows.

***

This trip to New York was unforgettable. It started off with a mini voyage for a concert. Max and the Girl drove to see Liza Minelli's concert in the Hollywood Bowl in Los Angeles, and afterwards the Girl was planning to take a red-eye flight to New York to enjoy an extra day in the city. She wanted to go to the Metropolitan museum and catch a show Sunday afternoon. Liza's concert wasn't spectacular, but she was a legend, and sometimes it's worth seeing legends just for the story-telling purposes. At the end of the concert, Liza announced that the song she was going to sing was dedicated to the memory of her long-time friend Marvin Hamlish. She also mentioned that she was going to attend his memorial service the next day.

"I won't be surprised if she's on the same plane with you. This memorial service is being held in New York in the morning, and your flight is one of the few flights that can make it there on time." Max informed her.

"I don't think Liza Minnelli will fly red-eye with me." The Girl has answered categorically.

She was definitely very surprised when several hours later in the airport, the woman who cut the line right in front of her ended up being from the Liza Minnelli team. Liza was sitting in a row of chairs by the window.

"You were right, Liza is here," the Girl texted Max right away.

"Get her autograph for me, please," he texted back.

The Girl didn't care for autographs or photos with celebrities. She believed that everyone should enjoy life, when they were off stage. However, what wouldn't you do for the man you love? She knew that Max would never forgive her for not taking advantage of the situation, and therefore, out of love to him, she had no choice. First she hesitated. It was very late; Liza did seem tired and in pain after the concert. As a result, while the Girl was standing in line and mulling it over, the Minnelli party had already left.

"Oh, well," she thought to herself with a sigh of relief. "I guess it wasn't meant to be."

But as soon as she walked through the gate, there was Liza, sitting comfortably in a chair next to the women's bathroom. This sight was so unexpected and genuine that now the Girl just couldn't resist, for the sake of the experience. *Seriously, how often do you see a legend sitting next to the bathroom in the airport?* The Girl came up to Liza, said thank you for a great concert, and asked for her autograph. "Use the ticket," Max instructed her via text. So she did: but instead of giving Liza her theater ticket, like Max wanted, she used her plane ticket to New York, and thus commemorated the obscurity of the whole scene. The Girl was even more astounded when, two hours later due to delays and plane cancellations, she left for New York on a different plane, while Liza and her party had to wait in the airport until the morning.

There wasn't enough space for everyone, but the Girl had been lucky enough to reregister right away. Somehow our perception of celebrities, regardless of their age and popularity, leads us to expect that they are never left behind like average human beings.

The purpose of this New York trip was multi-faceted. Universal Distributions had just hired a new sales manager, in addition to the other two hires on the operational side, when the super-woman assistant quit. The company was growing, and it was important to meet all together, to discuss growth issues and reset the office energy for the rest of the year. With all the new staff on board it was essential to create a sense of team unity, regardless of where the actual team members were located.

The Girl met with the new sales manager the same day she arrived. She visited the Metropolitan museum in the morning, and then she watched a Broadway show, had a nice dinner by herself, which always recharged her, and proceeded with informal introductions with this tiger of the industry. She insisted on meeting with him before the work week, because she felt that it was crucial for the management to act as a whole, like they already had an established bond. In other words, with all these new hires, they needed to walk into the office on Monday morning like collaborators in the company's success. Jake promised her that she was going to like the guy, and he was right. Strong, persistent, family-oriented, health-conscious, conservative, and firm in the decision making process, the new sales manager perfectly complemented Jake, and was an even more perfect addition to the company. *He strangely reminded the Girl of a noble combatant, who was not a leader by nature, but had the inner discipline to maintain long-lasting stability among his troops.* He just fit. The next three days in the office were spent in meetings, meetings, and more meetings. Everyone needed training, and given that the Girl was the only other person, besides Jake, who knew the ins and outs of the internal structure, there was a lot on her plate. But she loved every second of it. She was in her element, putting the pieces of the puzzle together on a bigger scale, supporting the company she loved, and working with people she whole-heartedly enjoyed. The whole team was fairly young, and the informal setup of the company made their interactions fun. The challenges made her brain spin at a fast speed, which was natural to her, interlacing problem-solving skills with openness to the exploration of unconventional solutions. She had learned long ago that *every problem always has a solution. It's just that solutions often are not obvious.* She loved the hunt for imperceptible but simple resolutions; she received an adrenalin boost from this process. Every day of this trip she walked into the office as if she belonged there. Unlike prior trips, she was no longer searching for her place within Universal Distributions. She had learned her place in this company deep in her gut. And, just as she knew that this was a temporary position, she knew how vital this position was for the current company situation, and she was happy with it. She carried out her role with the utmost gratitude, respect, and devotion, which only she was capable of.

The whole trip was wholesome and amazing. But there was one particular meeting that became a fundamental footstep for the Girl, because it gave her the opportunity to reflect on the past two years of her life: on everything she did, felt, experienced, smiled and sobbed over in that time, and put it in perspective within her life as a whole. *These moments of flashback, when everything is arranged by the Universe with impeccable precision, make the whole journey worthwhile.*

It was a gorgeous August Monday afternoon. The weather was mild for New York standards, and the sun had just peaked out from the clouds. It had been a long and productive morning, and Jake, the Girl, and the new sales manager were starving, so they decided to move their meeting to a nearby Italian restaurant that was located right across from the office. Jake's partner joined them as well, and the majority of the lunch consisted of technical talk on the subjects of product, changes, updates, etc. The Girl didn't really need to actively participate in the conversation, so she naturally just tuned it out. Her mind went on yet another escapade of analysis and observation, but this time she was the subject of her own study. She looked at the men at the table: all three of them were an average of 10 years older than she, and a lot more experienced in their own industry, running multi-million dollar projects on a daily basis; yet she absolutely felt she belonged right next to them in this discussion. They were using a lot of highly technical jargon, and to that day the majority of it sounded like gibberish to her. Even though hypothetically she'd like to better understand the technical aspects of the product, realistically she didn't need to. She was able to design and maintain whatever was needed to bring them all to this point with very limited technical knowledge, and that was an amazing fact in itself. The Girl then looked around and her gaze rested outside, on a movie truck parked right across from the restaurant. Not only was she sitting at a lunch table with three sophisticated and highly professional businessmen, feeling absolutely natural and equal, but she was also sitting in the heart of Manhattan, wearing her favorite outfit: a dress/heels combination, knowing that tonight she would experiment again with New York, either going dancing, watching another show, wandering around the city, or just reading in a French bistro with a glass of Pinot Noir in her hand. Her mind then took her even further back, to the time when she was sitting by the fire pit at Alex's house, completely lost, thinking that her ability to experience and project excitement had left her forever. Now she was making decent money with a diversity of options and a solid understanding that she could do it again, if something went south. She wasn't making a lot of money yet (that would be the next stage of her development), but now she could support herself. She was going further and further back in her memory, trying to reassess everything that had happened to her: all accidents, chain reactions, coincidences. At what point in her life did she take the right turn? How many right turns did she really take? How was it that everything she had rejected so viciously before had brought her so much unexpected satisfaction now? How did she manage to get to this level despite, the affirmations of Walter Diggins about financial ceilings and hierarchical necessities? At what point was she so starkly true to herself that she learned to move in unison with the divine? Was it when she went for an interview with Jake? Or maybe when she had the guts to define the lines in her life? Or maybe even further back, when she decided to return to the accounting field because she realized that she couldn't bear seeing her strong man in such a despair? How did she—a young 28-year-old girl with no fancy education, a definite case of ADD, a strong-willed character, and an aching necessity to believe that everything happened for a reason—how did she end up here, in this restaurant in the middle of New York, with these men next to her? Did that happen for a reason as well? Whatever it was, it felt absolutely, incredibly, and superbly magical. With only exception: she was unwinding her own fairy tale by letting things and people come to her as they were meant to. And that made her heart shriek with excitement.

"What are you giggling about?" The sales manager inquired, looking at her a little baffled.

"Was I giggling?" The Girl didn't realize that her thoughts were reflected on her face. "Just... stuff, you know." She shrugged and rearranged her napkin.

A minute later, she looked back outside to the street, and all of a sudden her eyes focused on the movie truck. This could not have been planned. It was a raw coincidence, another sign of destiny, another answer from the Universe.

"See the sign on that truck outside?" She was sitting next to Jake, so she instinctively turned to him and touched his hand.

"Yeah, what about it?" He looked at her for a second, and then moved his gaze outside, perplexed.

"This is how I live my life!" She replied, lost in her thoughts again.

The movie truck was advertising an upcoming cartoon *ParaNorman*. The huge slogan across the truck proclaimed *"You don't become a hero by being normal."*

9

THE END.THE BEGINNING

It was November again. The Girl and Max were sitting out on the balcony of a private membership club, located on the 34th floor of a downtown high rise. They were looking out over the city, having drinks, and smoking a cigar. The membership club was part of the same building where Jake had his office when the Girl came for an interview, only one level higher. They had just recently joined this club for two completely separate reasons: The Girl wanted to enjoy this view on her own terms whenever she liked, and Max used it as a networking resource to grow BooXkeeping.

Max was a sexy smoker. He enjoyed every second of every inhalation like he was drawing in the whole world. And when he exhaled little circles of smoke playfully into the air, he was practically playing with the world itself, with the world that he had inhaled a moment ago. The Girl always loved to watch him smoke. He did it with such a natural grace and masculinity that it stopped time for her. When he decided to quit smoking cigarettes several years back, even though she knew that it was the right thing to do, deep in her heart she was disappointed. But cigars suited him just perfectly. It was the rare and authentic combination of his controlled gestures and the slow motion, strong drink, strong flavor, and absolute active relaxation of his body that made her gasp every time he put that cigar in his mouth. Other than a few more grey hairs, there wasn't a trace of the challenges of the past two years in his posture or his face. It wasn't the same Max she talked to two years ago in Starbucks. This man was confident and satisfied. He belonged here at this level, with this view, next to these people; he knew what he was, why he was here, and what he was capable of, and most importantly he was happy with it. She observed him with a hint of smile, in complete silence: obsessively careful not to spoil this precious view of him so frankly enjoying himself. Interesting, she thought to herself, *how two people can live together for many years, assume that they know every cell of each other's bodies, each corner of each other's minds, and yet a simple ritual like smoking a cigar can be so energetically charging that it feels borderline sexual every time it occurs.*

Usually, the Girl would join Max and share his cigar. But this time, her mind was floating outside the windows in the foggy city; millions of unstructured thoughts were pounding in the back of her head. She was sipping port (she preferred port or bourbon with a cigar), and reflected on everything that had happened since her last New York trip, and actually since the Starbucks incident two years ago. She felt that she was at the end point in her life, getting closer and closer to the finish line of this marathon. And it was crucial for her to understand on a deep level what she was feeling and why.

***

The high feeling never lasts for a long period of time. *In fact, after every high note, there is a hasty slide to a low point before everything bounces back to normal.* The Girl was no different in that sense.

After an August trip to New York full of hype and high pitch energy, the Girl had made a couple of potentially unsafe mistakes within Universal Distributions. Jake called her to complain. Then, a new controller was not picking up the pace as fast as everyone hoped for. On top of that, he made few transitional mistakes, and so she got another phone call from Jake, who was already upset at this point. As if that wasn't enough, the team wouldn't cooperate on the software implementation, and Jake called her again, frustrated and angry. Now she got two to three calls a week from him, all with a negative connotation, meaning that something was going wrong within the company, or someone on the team had made an error. Every time the Girl was required to answer why this or that had happened, like it was entirely and solely her responsibility to make sure those operations ran smoothly within the company.

The calls were tough and took a lot of positive effort to handle. She knew all too well the sources of Jake's frustration. It was his Circle of Blindness. He was well balanced inside; he had seen her result-driven performance before, so he trusted her with this process. However, he wasn't prone to other human reactions, and since already he couldn't remember the reality of where they started, but couldn't see the vision in shining splendor yet either, he was disturbed. She learned to accept these phone calls as a sign of progress. From prior experience, she knew that *during any transition there are five stages to progress: rejection, frustration, cooperation, unexpected joy, and ownership. The transition from rejection to cooperation is always the hardest. The transition from cooperation to the unexpected joy is the least recognized. And the final stage of moving from unexpected joy to ownership is the most satisfying.* It was just bad luck that everything that went wrong would direct negativity towards her. Or maybe it was yet another test by destiny, for her to see just how much more she could handle when the odds were not in her favor. Strangely, despite all the problems and issues with the software integration and trainings, she developed an inner assurance that everything would go right. At the same time, she felt an unfamiliar disconnection from Universal Distributions. It didn't feel personal anymore; it became a faceless object to her: a project with tasks and due dates reaching the final stages of completion. *It's that feeling when you just know that whatever you are working on is going to happen because you have built enough credibility with the Universe and God thus far by contributing continuous genuine effort to get the process rolling; and now it was pure man-made labor, the calculated art of the mind, the combination of logic and teamwork that were going to finish the process.*

And then, all of a sudden, everything clicked together, like a three dimensional puzzle. For the next four weeks the Girl was tying up the loose ends, but the phone was quiet. Jake hadn't called. In his world, this meant that everything was going right. In her world, she appreciated any feedback, positive and negative, but she realized that she would probably never get it: he wasn't going to call to appreciate the progress. After all, Jake was no hero, no god. He was a human being, a strong-willed man with his own habits. She reached out a few times but with no response, so she quit trying. She limited communication to business related e-mails, concise and to-the-point, and the rest of the information she needed to relay to him she did so through company employees. She was a little distressed with him being so one-sided in his communication, and appearing only when he needed her to clean up the mess.

The Girl felt that her role within Universal Distributions was slowly approaching the finishing stages, and would require renegotiation or closure in the near future. Yet she wasn't ready to give it up, because there was still too much personal pleasure and mental challenge tied with it. It was like an addiction, like an energetic tie. BooXkeeping, on the other hand, was steadily growing. The new employee caught on very fast, and the company operational process stabilized. But the Girl also realized all too well that the business had reached a stagnant point where it needed more of her attention, creativity, passion, and work ethic to take it further. But unlike Universal Distributions, the projects were not so fascinating, and their completion felt more like a routine (profitable) business than a heavy romance with the highs and lows of company growth. She was going in circles in her own mind trying to decide what to do.

The answer came in a very easy way, like most answers do. At the end of September, the Girl, Max, and their friend took a four day trip to the Grand

Canyon. Neither one of them had ever been there, and all three of them needed a way to disconnect and reflect internally, so this trip sounded perfect.

If you have never sat or stood on the edge of the Grand Canyon, you have never perceived nature in its magnificent grandness and eternity. It really makes you realize how little you are in comparison to the rest of the Universe, how unknowledgeable, inexperienced and tiny you emerge against this natural power. You comprehend that this site has witnessed more rains, snows, sunsets, sunrises, tears, and smiles than you can ever imagine. Every stone has a color, a story, a secret. And all of them together amount to thousands of years worth of history, compiled into a death-like silence, which prevails over the canyon at all times.

The Girl spent the greater part of the time sitting on the very rim of the Canyon with her legs hanging over the cliff, over the infinity of this site. She liked the feeling of being a small subject in the Universe. She wasn't afraid of heights; she wasn't afraid of being belittled by natural forces. In fact, it encouraged humbleness and spirituality in her; it reminded her that instead of fighting the world, it's important to embrace it with everything it has to offer.

The energy of the Grand Canyon reminded the Girl of Jake's: tremendously grounded, powerful, and timeless, but also to some extent stale and unanimated. And while she was extremely grateful for the opportunity to experience this energy, *it wasn't her energy. Her energy was powerful in its dynamics, in the vibrancy of its colors, and in the bottomless depth of its passion. She was like a wind that dwelled within this canyon, free to come and go whenever it wanted, bringing freshness on the way in, nesting in the eternity of the walls of the canyon while there, and stirring the order on the way out on a mission to make the windmills spin in another part of the world.* She felt that Universal Distributions drained her energetically; BooXkeeping drained her mentally. And here on this rim on a starry night, listening to the stillness of the darkness, she asked herself one last time what she was supposed to do. The answer came instantaneously from within, sharp as a needle: the answer, which she intuitively knew she would have to face at one point or another, but which she was desperately trying to avoid it because she also knew how much it would hurt. She needed to let go of Universal Distributions. It would free up the space in the existing ReVision Triangle to give her room to jump up to the next level with BooXkeeping and whatever else would come her way. Simple. Painful. Sad.

Jake called a week later, for the first time in seven weeks. The Girl was with a client when she saw a missed call. Her initial inclination was that he finally reached out to express how satisfied and possibly even thankful he was with the results of the transition, but instinctively she knew that it wasn't true. And as soon as she called him back, she knew within the first ten minutes of their conversation: this was the beginning of the end. He called to discuss phasing her out. She had expected this conversation for a while, and after her Grand Canyon trip, she was even trying to prepare herself for it. But she imagined that they would be having it in New York (they had planned earlier that she would go there for a few days in October for a checkup visit) face-to-face, which was always substantially easier. But Jake decided to discuss it over the phone right then. The conversation started, continued, and ended on an off-note. Instead of being appreciative, he was inquisitive about the hours she spent on the project, and adamant about the necessity of cutting expenses and thus cancelling her trip to New York. He bargained over what her future maintenance fee would be, and so on and so forth. She understood the concerns of the businessman in him, but there were human relations involved in the progress of business development that could not be contained in the form of numbers, and he was definitely missing the significance of the human factor right now. The whole time, the Girl had a surreal feeling that this person on the other side of the headset wasn't the Jake she knew, but rather a complete stranger she has never met, and quite possible would never care to know. Simultaneously, she sensed in her gut that he wasn't ready for this talk; he didn't think it through, it just happened, as one thing led to another in the course of the conversation. Closer to the last third of the conversation, Jake had probably recognized that the exchange was heading in the wrong direction, because he tried to straighten things up, smooth them with the notion of how grateful he was for all she did, and so on, but it was few minutes too late. Her heart has already shut the doors. They ended the call on a friendly, neutral note, but she couldn't get over this phone call. It hit her on a core level, and she was stuck with it. She knew how much love, effort, time, and brain power she has invested in Universal

Distributions in the last year and a half. She also realized how much more she had completed within the company versus what she was originally hired to do. Moreover, she maintained the integrity to never allow herself to abuse the powers that came with this position. So, objectively speaking, she did a clean, superb job with extraordinary results on the Universal Distributions project, and if anything, she should have earned a big performance bonus, not a pep-talk. Hearing Jake comment on her hours, occasional unavailability, or making clever remarks about her having a little too much fun in New York while she was there for business, was unbearable. It was not the fair judgment of a reasonable person, who based his opinions on either logic or gut feelings. It felt like spit in the face.

She went home and did some chores, trying to occupy her mind, to calm herself down, and to tell herself that it wasn't a big deal. It was a normal course of events within business. *Nothing personal, just business.* But after a long, dreadful evening and a sleepless night (during which she reviewed in her head every single detail of her contract, trying to see what she might have missed, to analyze, and to play devil's advocate), she looked herself in the mirror in the morning and accepted that she was lying to herself. To her, it wasn't just a big deal, it was a life-and-death question! And if she buried it inside of her, she would never want to see or hear from Jake again. Partially, out of her deep respect for him, she had to find the strength in her heart to open the door that was shut 16 hours ago and explain to him her side of things. But mostly, she needed to do it for her own sake, to stay true to herself, to not allow it to break her, to define the final traces of the lines that were left untouched, even if it would not lead anywhere.

So the Girl wrote Jake a long e-mail. She explained in a great detail how unhappy she was that the conversation happened over the phone, because while he found time and money to visit vendors and customers, he didn't think of the importance of meeting with one of the key people in his company to discuss these very crucial matters in person. She expressed her opinion on his one-sided communication: how he only reached out when everything was wrong, but she was stuck with his complete silence when everything was going well — and while this might have been OK in his world, it definitely wasn't acceptable in hers. She proceeded with the notion that his scrutinizing of her hours felt like a punch, spit in the face, because if they were to go back and recalculate her hours based on their original verbal contract, he would end up owing her money, not the other way around. She continued with the fact that bargaining over her future maintenance contract, on top of everything else, was just cheap. And moreover, she addressed his comments on how she had fun in New York while she was there on business trips with the statement that she never played there at his expense. In fact, she worked 12-13 hour days to achieve what they had achieved, but what she did between the end of the workday and the beginning of a next workday was her own business. She happened to love life, to seize and enjoy every moment she could, and she wasn't planning on spending her nights in a hotel room watching TV, just because she was there on business.

She ended her e-mail with the following words.

"I have always been honest with you, Jake, and I take pride for that in our business and personal relationship. Therefore it was important for me that you have a clear understanding of what is really going on here and how I felt yesterday. To get there, I needed to write this e-mail. Now I feel OK and complete regarding our conversation yesterday. Thank you!"

She didn't expect an answer at all. She was almost hopeful that he would miss it, as he often did with the work e-mails. But the answer came back within few hours.

"I'm glad you feel OK and complete :)", he wrote. *"And I do love and appreciate you like you will never know, I guess."*

"Then, going forward," she was quick to respond, "don't ever deprive yourself of the inclination to tell me how much you love and appreciate me the way you really do. I'll learn to understand."

"I have a feeling you already did." Was Jake's instant reply.

***

Letting go is the most complicated of human processes. The reason is straightforward: if you stay true to yourself, you embed a part of yourself into everything or everyone that you touch and come across. You can't control it; you just exchange energies. In the same way, that other person embeds part of himself in you. Therefore, when you need to let go of a person, event, or object, you are really just leaving behind that part of yourself that was embedded in the subject of letting go, like a ballast, in order to move forward. But letting go of a part of yourself inevitably inflicts internal pain, and takes time to heal.

That November night, on the 34th floor, with a glass of port in her hand, the Girl was recapping, reiterating her experiences and feelings. It had been seven weeks since that final e-mail and conversation with Jake. In the beginning the pain was sharp; she could sense the immediate changes within Universal Distributions since she was no longer a part of it. And she felt terribly alone and numb in this process of letting go; she couldn't share it with anybody, this almost romantic involvement with the project, because no one would understand it the way it really was. She reminded herself daily that this pain was a temporary thing and she just needed to work through it. With time, as she moved into the maintenance stage of the contract and trained her brain not to care in the way she did before, the pain had dulled, and consequently went away, leaving a big void where there used to be a passion for Universal Distributions' success. Meanwhile, BooXkeeping had picked up almost immediately. It was as if it were waiting for her commitment, for the concentration of her free time and energy. Freddie was an amazing source of references, and though the growth was still in the linear stage, it was definitely heading in an exponential direction. So ultimately, she knew she had done the right thing.

If she could structure what she had learned throughout the personal and professional journey of the last two years in lessons, she would do so in the following manner:

#1: When you keep your mind open, it picks up the books, movies, songs, shows, ideas, and people that the subconscious needs the most at that particular moment. As the saying goes, God doesn't give us what we want, he gives us what we need.

#2: Complete darkness wakes up passive or secondary senses and skills. It's empowering.

#3: There no good or bad ideas: some are viable, some are not; some are within context, and some are outside of the business realm — but maybe only temporarily.

#4: Define the lines early on. It will save time and effort.

#5: Stay flexible and inquisitive. Remember: every problem always has a solution. Sometimes the solution is not obvious. Keep searching.

#6: You are what you are. No more, no less. Embrace it.

If anyone ever tells you a story with a happy or a sad end, don't believe them, because they are not telling a full story. Someone once said that *everything's OK in the end, if it's not OK, it's not the end.*

The state of OK is neither high nor low: it's neutral.

The Girl turned to Max, who was enthusiastically chatting with a man he met at a networking breakfast, and fixed her eyes on him for few seconds. He seemed his cheerful self. But was she happy? Had she achieved her vision? They had reached their financial breaking point right before the end of the Universal Distributions contract, which now had decreased significantly in its fee, and so they were in the process of getting more clients to go above and beyond their financial goal. The good news was that the process was finally setup correctly because it provided security in funds due to diversity in the client list. Through trial and error, she had created a workplace where she fit, where she didn't have to prove to anybody the credibility of her resume at her young age, where she could have just as much or as little structure as she wanted in order to operate. Her relationship with Max had strengthened and deepened, which was an added bonus to the whole process, but they still had occasional arguments, like all others, which kept the relationship real. She wasn't sure where she wanted to go from here, or how to get there once she knew, so she was slightly agitated. But overall, she was OK, in all aspects of her life. *She was content.*

Except for one element, that was gradually eating her up.

***

"Alex, why do I feel empty?" She asked him, without saying hello again. She had called him right after she and Max got back from the club. It was 10:40pm.

"Because you need to learn to be proud of your accomplishments." He answered in a casual manner, as if she was asking him what kind of sandwich he wanted for lunch. He anticipated this question. *"You didn't steal any of your accomplishments, you didn't deserve them, you didn't beg for them either. You earned them: now you need to own them."*

"Are you saying that I am so fucked up that I can't even be proud of myself?"

"You are not fucked up, you are *unique*. You have a clash in your internal definition, which is a common occurrence. But it is exactly this deviation in definition that rules the emptiness in you instead of filling the same space with a deep and colorful satisfaction with your own achievements."

"May be I need to go skydiving again," she said, mostly to herself, after his simple but profound statement. Alex was making sense on a logical level, but whatever it was that he meant didn't click internally. "May be I just need another reboot and everything is going to fall into place."

"You don't need a reboot, you need an upgrade," he said, and then added. "I'll pick you up on Wednesday. Don't jump until then."

Wednesday was her birthday.

"Happy Birthday," he said as soon as she opened the car door, and gave her a big hug.

"You know, somehow I never liked my birthday." She stated kissing him on the cheek. She couldn't get rid of the stupid numbness inside, which irritated her, so she didn't feel like talking.

"I think your attitude will change after today," Alex replied, and began a conversation, but she was hardly participating. She felt weirdly absent. She was hushed for the majority of the ride, half-absorbed in her own thoughts, half-listening to him.

When they exited the freeway and pulled away from the main road, she realized that she never asked where he was taking her.

"Where are we going?" She turned her head back and tried to look inside of the trunk of his Porsche to find any clues to their destination.

"You have mastered the skill of high jump in your life. You have also learned to spread your wings. Now it's time you start flying." He said with a puzzling smile, pulling into the glider port.

The glider port was situated on a cliff by the ocean. It was a beautiful, chilly day, and while it was sunny, the sky was still full of heavy clouds.

"You know, you had a 50/50 chance of being able to paraglide today due to the weather conditions," Alex mentioned in a matter-of-fact way. "But somehow you always pull it off."

"I don't pull it off," she thought. "I just stay true to myself and my Universe replies to me in a timely fashion."

She felt the breeze touching her face and her skin. The paragliding pilots were carrying their equipment, spreading it on the ground, cleaning, getting ready for a takeoff. She overheard an old man talking to two visitors "This is as close as you can get to flying without growing your own wings." Right now the emptiness inside her made everything feel like it was ending. But the end of something is always the beginning of something new. In a few minutes she would be up there in the sky with the rest of the pilots, and maybe, just maybe, that would mark the beginning of a new and exciting period for her, and most importantly, it would fill this growling void.

She remembered the song she had heard five days ago at the California Adventure Park. The song was from a new animation film she hadn't seen yet. Five days ago, she had no understanding of the message behind this song and what it meant for her, or why it caught her attention. Now it made an absolute sense.

When the cold wind is calling
And the sky is clear and bright
Misty mountains sing and beckon,
"Lead me out into the light"

I will ride, I will fly
Chase the wind and touch the sky
I will fly
Chase the wind and touch the sky

Where dark woods hide secrets
And mountains are fierce and bold
Deep waters hold reflections
Of times lost long ago

I will hear their every story
Take hold of my own dream
Be as strong as the seas are stormy
And proud as an eagle's scream

I will ride, I will fly

Chase the wind and touch the sky
I will fly
Chase the wind and touch the sky.

("Touch the Sky," *Brave*, 2012)

Twenty minutes later, a young, tan man was buckling her into the gear, getting her ready for a flight.

"What's your name?" He asked her.

"Girl. What's yours?" She asked him back.

"Max." He answered.

"Max?" She couldn't believe her ears. "How funny!" She added without a trace of a smile on her face.

It was indeed candidly ironic, that the man who pushed her into this ReVision triangle and the man who was about to pull her out of it into another level of her life had an identical name. Another coincidence, or a planned act of the Universe and God together?

EPILOGUE

The first few seconds of flight are accompanied by a very sad feeling. I am doing this alone. Alone again. Here I am, 29 years later, leaving everything and everybody behind and moving forward by myself. Feels like a waste of time and effort, right? Wrong. In a minute the sad and lonely feeling is gone. You come into this world alone, you leave it alone. And all major shifts happen only when you are truly alone. A little sad to leave, a little excited for the unknown, slightly scared that in a way you have no idea what is going to come out of this step, yet no regrets, because everything at the prior dimension has been exhausted. And there is no way to feel it unless you are completely and utterly on your own.

Unique equals free. No other way. I always felt like a puzzle with a missing piece, but today I feel that my puzzle is complete, it's just that its shape is an uneven octagon with rounded edges. This is what my world feels like: open and free. It's detached from the Earth, but not by much. Sometimes, I ride a little higher, other times, I sink below the level of what seems to be the ground. Often I ride on a parallel level and occasionally I even step on the ground to take a rest, look around, and figure out a new direction. I can see other people far or near; yet I remain an observer because many can't see my face from the distance: to them I am just a stranger who is passing by in their lives. As long as I bring no harm, they don't mind. And the beauty of this phenomenon is when they don't feel that they are being observed, they are comfortable and safe to stay true to themselves, to keep dancing, kissing, working, or dreaming in their homes with the people they love and the possessions they treasure, which makes observation even more beautiful and meaningful. Just like birds, I move faster than many other living creatures of my kind, but it's my speed and it feels right. I am not competing or chasing after what doesn't belong to me. I live my life at my pace, on my ground rules, and by my laws. I love whoever I want to love. I do whatever I want to do. I feel whatever I want to feel. I create whatever I want to create. I make whatever I can make. And on these terms, I fit in both my world, and ultimately in the bigger world, with 6.5 billion of other people. Though my world is just a little part of this big world, everything in it is designed and built by and for me, so even the tiniest corner feels right. Every passing person feels like he was meant to visit me, to teach me some small or great lesson in my lifetime, and every experience makes me grow in an interesting and compelling way. In this world, I belong. Here I am loved and appreciated. Here I don't need to be normal, different, or special. I just am.

Unconditional freedom is neither rich nor poor, neither sad nor happy, neither good nor bad, neither mental nor physical, neither silent nor loud, neither deep nor shallow. It's in its own league. This freedom is dynamic, cool, clear, and content; it sounds like the wind, and it feels like flying. This freedom is unique and powerful. So am I.

And with this approach, the sky is no limit. Therefore it's time for the exploration of new dimensions, a new ReVision Triangle.

Vision accomplished.

ELENA EMMA

www.ingramcontent.com/pod-product-compliance
Lightning Source LLC
LaVergne TN
LVHW051101080426
835508LV00019B/1996